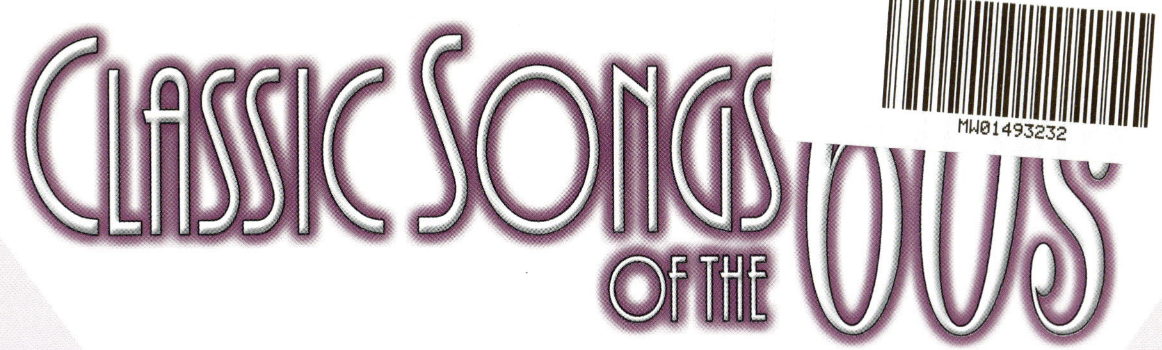

Project Manager: Carol Cuellar

Text By: Fucini Productions, Inc.

Cover Design: Joseph Klucar

Art Layout: Martha L. Ramirez

Production Coordinator: Donna Salzburg

Contents

Introduction

Revolutionary. If we could pick only one word to describe the '60s, this would be it. During these ten turbulent years, many of our preconceived notions about government, society, family, and culture were suddenly turned upside down. The United States became mired in a war in a far-off land called Vietnam, a country that very few Americans had even heard of a decade earlier. Racial tensions flared, and sections of cities from Newark to Los Angeles went up in flames. A president was assassinated, and then his alleged gunman was himself shot before our very eyes on national television.

The birth control pill sparked the "sexual revolution." Women's skirts kept getting shorter, and men's hair grew ever longer. Ordinary people in average American towns began experimenting with drugs, dropping out of their old lives, moving into communes, and joining protest marches.

Meanwhile, technology moved ahead at a breathtaking pace. Doctors performed the first human heart transplants and implanted the first artificial hearts in patients. Early photocopying machines and computers began appearing in more offices. We not only traveled into outer space, but also by the end of the decade we had actually walked on the moon.

Technology was also changing the world of music in the '60s. Robert Moog invented the Moog synthesizer, ushering in the era of electronic music. The monaural recordings of earlier decades had given way to stereo, and FM had replaced AM as the primary radio band.

The music of the '60s often reflected the uncertainty of these uproarious times. Some songs from early in the decade, such as Del Shannon's "Runaway" (1961), which featured Max Crook's surreal and haunting solo on the Musitron synthesizer, seem to foreshadow the tumultuous events that lay ahead in the '60s. Powered by Shannon's evocative guitar playing and vocals, "Runaway" went on to become a runaway hit, selling 80,000 copies a day at one point and reaching the top of the charts.

On the other hand, many great songs of the '60s offered a welcome break from the turmoil of the decade. Sure, the times seemed chaotic, but listening to these songs, you could reassure yourself that this was just society's way of righting old wrongs and working out new values. Things would sort themselves out soon enough. Meanwhile, why not enjoy the sweet harmonies of the Drifters singing "Under the Boardwalk," the Association's sentimental ballad "Never My Love," or a lighthearted song like "The Lion Sleeps Tonight"? A No.1 hit from the Tokens in 1961, this famous doo-wop tune was taken from "Mbube," a South African folk song.

As it had throughout history, music served two very different purposes in the '60s. It offered people a chance to express their deepest and most disquieting feelings while at the same time providing them with a means of escaping into pure flights of harmonic fantasy. So savor this '60s musical sampler. We think you'll agree that in addition to tie-dyed shirts and lava lamps, this momentous decade produced some of the most memorable songs of all time.

Gimmicks and Greatness

Rock 'n' roll had clearly established itself as the dominant form of popular music by the early '60s. Perhaps this gave rock artists the confidence to relax and inject an element of humor into their work. For whatever reason, the '60s witnessed an explosion of spoof songs that served up great music with a lighthearted twist.

Among the most popular of these songs was Johnny Rivers' "Secret Agent Man," which played on the James Bond craze of the '60s. Rivers' sharp tenor voice and understated lead guitar made this slightly tongue-in-cheek tune about a "man who leads a life of danger" one of the decade's most recognizable hits.

The biggest dance craze of the '60s arrived on the scene early in the decade. In August 1960, a young singer from Philadelphia named Chubby Checker released a song called "The Twist." Within seven weeks, the song reached the top of the charts as people of all ages were gyrating and bending to the driving rhythms of the new dance.

Americans kept twisting for more than two years. Checker's original version of "The Twist" actually reached No. 1 on two separate occasions. For good measure, the singer also had a major hit with "Let's Twist Again."

Although the twist can be described as a "fad," both the song and the dance had much deeper implications. With its fast beat, "The Twist" inspired a new sound that dominated rock 'n' roll in the early '60s before the British Invasion. The popularity of the twist also changed our ideas about dancing. Unlike earlier dances, which required a partner, anyone could enjoy the twist dancing alone. As an individualized free-wheeling form of expression, the twist fit perfectly into the do-your-own-thing philosophy of the '60s.

The twist was also the first rock 'n' roll phenomenon to attract large numbers of adults. Within a year of the dance's introduction, adult establishment figures like the Duke and Duchess of Bedford, Oleg Cassini, and even the great Greta Garbo could be seen twisting the night away at fashionable nightclubs. By enticing so many prominent figures onto the dance floor, the twist brought rock 'n' roll a new level of respectability.

In addition to ushering in new fads, the '60s was the defining decade for some of the greatest musical geniuses in the history of rock 'n' roll. It was in this decade that Dion DiMucci left the Belmonts to establish his own career as a solo performer with hits like "The Wanderer" and "Runaround Sue."

The great Roy Orbison, who would influence so many future superstars from Tom Petty to Bruce Springsteen, found his voice in the '60s. Orbison had eight Top 10 hits between 1960 and 1964. His breakthrough song "Only the Lonely" (1960), with its melancholy feel and glass-shattering falsetto, established Orbison as one of the most evocative and gifted artists of all time.

"Only the Lonely" reached No. 2 in the U.S. and No. 1 in Great Britain. Ironically, Orbison almost gave this landmark ballad away before he recorded it. At six o'clock one morning, he delivered the song to Elvis Presley, but the superstar was still sleeping. Not wishing to wait around, Orbison tried interesting the Everly Brothers in his tune, but they turned him down. Finally, he recorded it himself, launching an internationally acclaimed career. As people would have said in the '60s, this ironic series of events proved to be "good karma" for rock 'n' roll fans everywhere.

Girls Rule

With few exceptions, female artists stayed in the shadows during the early years of rock 'n' roll, typically performing as background singers or part of a male-dominated group. This all began to change in the '60s, the decade that spawned the modern Women's Lib movement.

Almost from the beginning of the decade, the '60s brought us a new generation of "girl groups." Bold and confident, these young artists were unapologetic in addressing issues from a woman's perspective in their music. The style and substance of their songs enriched rock 'n' roll, making it more complete.

Among the earliest girl groups was the Shirelles, from Passaic, New Jersey. Paving the way for future women rockers, the Shirelles became the first all-female group to have a No. 1 record. The group's 1962 hit "Baby It's You," which reached No. 8 on the charts, showcased their harmonic talents. This song, with its famous "sha la la la la" refrain, was later covered by an up-and-coming group called the Beatles.

Around the same time that the Shirelles were rewriting rock history, the Crystals were also making waves with rough-edged songs like "He's a Rebel" that smashed the stereotypical image of the feminine sound.

Girl groups weren't the only female artists tearing up the charts. In 1963, Lesley Gore, a fresh-faced 17-year-old from New Jersey, had a No.1 hit with the Quincy Jones-produced song "It's My Party." Gore followed this hit with other perky tunes. Then in 1964, she showed another, more intense side of her musical gifts by releasing "You Don't Own Me." A defiant affirmation of a young woman's right to her own identity in a relationship, "You Don't Own Me" reached No. 2 on the charts and foreshadowed the feminist songs of a future generation.

The '60s also saw the emergence of two of the most gifted female vocalists in the history of pop music—Dusty Springfield and Aretha Franklin. Born Mary O'Brien in London, the girl who would become the legendary Dusty Springfield grew up in Britain's folk and pop scene. She began her career with a group called the Lana Sisters before joining her brother in the Springfields.

In 1963, Springfield struck out on her own, releasing the groundbreaking hit "I Only Want to Be With You," which reached the top of the charts on both sides of the Atlantic. With its bold, brassy horns and fast tempo, the song seemed to herald the arrival of a major new star. Throughout her glorious career, Springfield more than lived up to this early expectation.

The daughter of a Detroit minister, Aretha Franklin began singing in her father's New Bethel Baptist Church choir at the age of 12. From the very beginning, it became apparent that Franklin was blessed with a divine voice of unparalleled power. Infusing energy and rhythm into every lyric, Franklin has an unmatched ability to turn even the simplest melody into a moving and uplifting experience.

Under Franklin's influence, the rock and pop music of the '60s took on a spiritual passion. Like few other vocalists before, or since, the dynamic diva from Detroit seemed to master her voice as an instrument, driving it from throaty growls through swoops and dives to lighthearted flights of fancy. On June 28, 1968, Franklin appeared on the cover of *Time* magazine. The "Queen of Soul" was officially crowned, and rock 'n' roll music would never be the exclusive domain of males again.

British Invasion

On July 20, 1957, a young British guitarist asked the 15-year-old son of a bus driver to join the Quarrymen, a skiffle band he had formed a few years earlier. The bus driver's son agreed—and the history of popular music would never be the same. The guitarist was John Lennon and the 15-year-old was Paul McCartney, and by the early '60s, the Quarrymen were knocking fans from Liverpool to Hamburg off of their feet under a new name—the Beatles.

The Beatles officially came into being in the final form that everyone recognizes in August 1962, when drummer Ringo Starr joined Lennon, McCartney, and George Harrison. By the time they disbanded eight years later, the group had recorded 214 songs, made five films, shattered virtually all recording-industry sales records, and helped define the sensibilities of an entire generation.

Mixing youthful exuberance with skillful musicianship, and sophisticated harmonies with refreshingly original melodies and lyrics, the Beatles gave rock 'n' roll a shot of creative energy and vitality that had been missing since the days of Buddy Holly. The group's roots in a rough Irish working-class section of Liverpool gave the Beatles an aura of outsider rebelliousness that resonated with young people on both sides of the Atlantic during the uneasy '60s. Yet at the same time, the four shaggy-haired young men had an undeniable charm and infectious humor that made it easy to feel comfortable with them.

It was this mixture of the rough and the gentle, of the mysterious outsiders and the friendly boys next door, that made the Beatles so immensely popular. They embodied the complexity of the '60s and turned it into beautiful music. This is evident in their first American No. 1 hit, "I Want to Hold Your Hand." Lennon and McCartney wrote this song while sitting together at a piano in the basement of Paul's girlfriend's house. The young composers packed a sweeping array of harmonies, melodies, and hand-clapping into this song, which they recorded in October 1963 at Abbey Road on the studio's new four-track equipment.

"I Want to Hold Your Hand" was released the day after Christmas in 1963. It quickly reached No. 1 in the U.S. and remained there for seven weeks. Although this was the Beatles' first American chart-topper, the group had scored its first No. 1 in the UK in May 1963 with "From Me to You."

The success of the Beatles paved the way for other great British bands in the '60s, including another Liverpool group, Gerry & the Pacemakers. Formed by Gerry Marsden and his brother Freddie, the Pacemakers pioneered the Mersey sound (as celebrated in their song "Ferry Across the Mersey"). The group's first single, "How Do You Do It," reached No. 1 in the UK, as did their second song, "I Like It."

In March 1964, the Dave Clark Five seemed poised to challenge the Beatles in America when their hard-driving "Glad All Over" became a runaway hit. The Hollies racked up 16 Top 10 hits in the UK but weren't quite as successful in the U.S. However, the group's upbeat and harmonious "Carrie-Ann" was one of the biggest American hits of 1967. Eric Burdon and the Animals brought a more bluesy twist to British music with songs like "House of the Rising Sun." Another British group, Herman's Hermits, served up a softer variety of music. Between 1964 and 1967, they had 11 Top 10 hits, including "Mrs. Brown You've Got a Lovely Daughter."

A different, more subtle British sound was offered by the Zombies. Their bouncy chord progressions, frequent use of minor keys, and breathless vocals foreshadowed the more complex rock of a later era. "She's Not There," the Zombies' first single, reached No. 2 on the U.S. charts.

The British Invasion may have been dominated by the towering figures of the Beatles, but as groups like the Animals, Herman's Hermits, and the Zombies showed, the new musical phenomenon offered Americans a dazzling array of new, and very different, sounds.

Beyond the Beatles

The Beatles and other British groups dominated the rock scene for much of the mid-'60s. However, as the decade progressed, American artists reasserted themselves with innovative pop-rock and folk-rock sounds that set the standard for future generations of musicians.

This change in American pop coincided with a shift in the center of the music scene from New York to California in the mid-'60s. For many music fans, the wild success of the Mamas & the Papas seemed to epitomize this coast-to-coast relocation. The group grew out of the New York folk-music scene of the early '60s. With success eluding them in Manhattan, the group's four members—John Phillips, Michelle Phillips, Denny Doherty, and Ellen Naomi Cohen (Cass Elliott)—left for the warmer and friendlier confines of Los Angeles.

In 1966, less than a year after arriving on the West Coast, the Mamas & the Papas had their first big hit, "California Dreamin'." With its evocative blend of tight harmonies, haunting lyrics, flutes, and acoustic guitars, the song mixed elements of jazz and folk with rock 'n' roll to create a lively new American sound.

Able to bridge divergent musical and cultural tastes, "California Dreamin'" received plenty of air time on mainstream AM radio stations while still attracting a large following of fans among underground FM listeners. The counterculture mood that ran through the song gave many AM fans their first exposure to the growing hippie movement and foreshadowed the Summer of Love that lay on the horizon.

Another fresh new sound burst upon the pop scene in the mid-'60s when the Fifth Dimension recorded a remake of the Mamas & the Papas tune "Go Where You Wanna Go." Released in 1966, this was the first Top 20 hit for the incredibly talented group that would become known the world over for its soaring harmonies and deft blend of sophisticated pop and soul sounds.

Like the Mamas & the Papas and the Fifth Dimension, Sonny & Cher also brought a new level of excitement and complexity to American pop music in the post-British Invasion '60s. Salvatore "Sonny" Bono was a moderately successful songwriter in the early '60s when he met and fell in love with a young aspiring singer named Cherilyn Sarkisian LaPierre ("Cher").

In 1965, the couple released their recording of Sonny's sentimental love song, "I Got You Babe." The song's easy rhythm, underscored by innovative organ music and inventive duet parts, helped make it one of the biggest hits of the year.

Touring to promote their smash single, Sonny & Cher were frequent guests on radio and TV programs. Their charismatic personalities and colorful bell-bottom-and-vest mode of dress attracted people to the growing youth culture of the '60s. Later in the decade, Sonny & Cher's music took on an edgier tone as they explored more topical themes, as evidenced in the social commentary hit "The Beat Goes On."

In so doing, the couple joined groups like the Mamas & the Papas and the Fifth Dimension to give pop music a new and deeper meaning, making it more truly reflective of life during this eventful decade.

Things That First Appeared in the '60s

1. Men on the moon
2. Love beads
3. Peace symbols
4. The computer mouse
5. Freeze-dried coffee
6. Laser eye surgery
7. NutraSweet
8. Hand-held calculators
9. Domed stadiums
10. Permanent-press fabrics
11. ATMs
12. Touch-tone phones

(THERE'S) ALWAYS SOMETHING THERE TO REMIND ME

Words by
HAL DAVID

Music by
BURT BACHARACH

C9
Am/C
C7
F
calls how much in love we used to be.
how it felt to kiss and hold you tight. Oh, how can
where we used to go and I'll be there.
C/E
G7/D
C7
C7sus
C7
I for - get you, when there is al - ways some - thing there
F
C
C7
C7sus
C7
to re - mind me; Al - ways some - thing there
F
C
Em7
to re - mind me. I was born to

Am7
Fmaj7
love you and I will nev - er be
G
(tacet)
C
free. You'll al - ways be a part of me. Wo wo
1. 2.
3.
wo.
wo.
C
Repeat and Fade
I'll nev - er love an - oth - er, ba - by.
I nev - er will for - get you, ba - by.
You'll al - ways be a part of me, oh.

ANYONE WHO HAD A HEART

Words by
HAL DAVID

Music by
BURT BACHARACH

D♭
E♭
take me in his arms and love me
A♭
Cm7
too. You could-n't real-ly have a heart and
hurt me like you hurt me and be so un-
C
Am
Am7
true. What am I to do?
Ev-'ry time you go a-way, I al-ways say

Fmaj7
B♭sus
B♭
Am
Am7
this time it's good-bye, dear.
Lov-ing you the way I do, I take you back;
Fmaj7
B♭sus
B♭
F
E♭
With-out you I'd die, dear.
Know-ing I love you
A♭
Cm7
so.
An-y-one who had a heart would
D♭
E♭
D♭
E♭
D♭
E♭
D♭
E♭
take me in his arms and love me

A♭
Cm7
too. You could-n't real-ly have a heart and
D♭
E♭
hurt me like you hurt me and be so un-
1. A♭
C
2. A♭
F
true. What am I to do?
true. Any-one who had a heart would love me
you.
A♭
F
D♭maj7
Cm7
D♭
too. Any-one who had a heart would sure-ly take me in his arms and al-ways

D♭maj7
Cm7
B♭m7
E♭
A♭
F
love me, Why won't you?
An - y - one who had a heart would love me
too.
An - y - one who had a heart would sure - ly
fade out
take me in his arms and al - ways love me, Why won't
D♭

BABY, IT'S YOU

Words and Music by
BURT BACHARACH, MACK DAVID
and BARNEY WILLIAMS

C
la.
It's not the way you kiss that tears me a -
They say, they say you've nev-er,nev-er,nev-er, ev - er been
G
(2nd time)
Cheat!
Cheat!
part.
true.
Oh, oh,
Oh, oh,
Em
1. many-y, man-y many nights go by,
2. & 3. does-n't mat-ter what they say,
Am
I sit a - lone at home and I cry o - ver
I know I'm gon-na love you an - y old way, what can I

G
Em
you;
what can I do?
do,
when it's true?
C
D7
Ah
Can't help my - self,
Don't want no - bod-y no - bod- y,
N.C.
'cause ba - by, it's
G 6/9
Em
Sha la la la la la la.
3rd time to Coda
Sha la la la la la
you.
Ba - by, it's
you.
1. Em
la.
Sha la la la
2. Em
la.
C
3
Solo guitar 15va lower

D
G
C
D
G
D.S. al Coda
Oh, oh
CODA
G 6/9
Em
G 6/9
Sha la la la la la la.
Sha la la la la la
you.
Don't leave me all a -
lone,
Em
G 6/9
Em
G
la.
Sha la la la la la la.
come on home
'cause ba - by it's you.
(Fading out)

THE BIRDS AND THE BEES

Words and Music by
HERB NEWMAN

G
way they could kiss,
on a night _ like
this.
G7
C
When I look in - to your big brown eyes
G
it's so ver - y plain to see
Em7
A7
that it's time you learned _ a - bout the

D7 Am7 D7

facts of life__ start - ing from "A" to "Z". Let me tell ya 'bout the

G D7

birds and the bees and the flow - ers and the trees and the moon up a-bove

1 G

and a thing__ called love.__

2 G Am7 Gmaj7

Let me tell ya 'bout the love.__

THE BEAT GOES ON

Words and Music by
SONNY BONO

Verse
C7
1. Charles - ton was once the rage, uh - huh,
2. The groc - 'ry store does su - per mart, uh - huh,
3. Grand-mas sit in chairs and rem - i - nisce,
mp
His - to - ry has turned a page, uh - huh.
Lit - tle girls still break their hearts, uh - huh.
Boys keep chas - ing girls to get a kiss.
The
And
The
min - i - skirt's the cur - rent thing, uh - huh,
men still keep on march - ing off to war,
cars keep go - ing fast - er all the time,
Last time D. S. and fade
Teen - y bop-per is our new born king, uh huh,
'Lec - tric - 'ly they keep their base-ball score,
Bums still cry, "Hey bud - dy have you got a dime,
and The Beat Goes On

BLUE ANGEL

Words and Music by
ROY ORBISON and
JOE MELSON

Chorus 2:
We'll have love so fine,
Magic moments divine.
If you'll just say you're mine,
I'll love you 'til the end of time.
Don't you worry your pretty head;
I'll never let you down.
I'll always be around,
Blue Angel.

BLUE VELVET

Words and Music by
BERNIE WAYNE and LEE MORRIS

Cm
F7
B♭
Dm
She wore blue vel - vet,
Cm7
F7(♭9)
B♭
Cm7
blu - er than vel - vet were her eyes,
warm - er than May her ten-der
F7
Fm7
sighs, love was ours.
B♭9
E♭
(appassionato)
E♭m7
Ours, a love I held tight - ly,
ff
(appassionato)

B♭ B♭7

feel - ing the rap - ture grow,

E♭ E♭m7 Dm7 D♭dim7

like a flame burn - ing bright - ly. But when she left,

Cm7 F7 B♭ Dm

rit. *a tempo*

gone was the glow of blue vel - vet.

Cm7 F7(♭9) B♭ Cm7

But in my heart there'll al-ways be, pre - cious and warm, a mem-o -

F7
Fm
ry through the years,
B♭9
E♭
F7(♯5)
molto espressivo
and I still can see blue vel - vet through my
mp
subito molto espressivo
rit.
1.
2.
B♭6
G7(♭9)
Cm
F7
B♭6
a tempo
tears.
She wore
tears.
a tempo
mf

BUILD ME UP BUTTERCUP

Words and Music by
TONY McCAULEY and
MICHAEL D'ABO

C
E7(♯5)
of all (worst of all) you nev - er call ba - by when you
F
G11
say you will (say you will) but I love you still; I need you
C
G7
C7
(I need you) more than an - y - one dar - ling you
F
Fm
E7(♯5)
Fm6
C
know that I have from the start. So build me up (build me up) but -

To Coda
G7
F
C
Dm7
C
G
- ter - cup don't break my heart.
I'll be
To
C
G
B♭
F
ov - er at ten, you tell me time and a - gain but you're late,
you I'm a toy but I could be the boy you a - dore.
C
Dm
Dm9
G7
C
G
I wait a - round and then: I run to the door, I can't take
If you just let me know: and though you're un - true I'm at - tract -
B♭
F
C
Dm
C
an - y more, it's not you, you let me down a - gain.
- ed to you all the more why do I need you so?

Dm
Dm
G7
C
Dm
Em
Ba - by ba - by
try to find
a lit - tle time and
A7
Dm
A7
Dm
D7
I'll make you hap - py, I'll be home, I'll be be - side the 'phone, wait - ing for
3
2nd time D.S. al Coda
G
Gsus
G13
G9sus
G13
G11
G9sus
G13
you.
Oo
Oo
Why do you
f
CODA
F
C
Dm7
C
Don't break my heart.
R.H.
L.H.

CANDY MAN

Words and Music by
NEIL FREDERICKS and
BEVERLY ROSS

C7
G
hon-ey let me be
all your own can - dy,
can - dy,
your can - dy man.
G7
G♯7
A7
D
Well, hey there sweet thing.
I love your hon-ey lov - in' ways.
D7
Hey there sweet
G7
thing,
I love your hon-ey lov - in',

D
hon-ey lov-in' ways.
So come to me,
A7
G7
and I'll let you be
all my own
D
can - dy, can - dy,
my can - dy man.
A7
D
N.C.
G/D
Come on
wom-an,
I'm gon-na treat you right.
D N.C.
G/D
D N.C.
D7
I'll give you can - dy kiss - es
ev-'ry sin - gle night,

G7
G
so come on, ba - by,
I love your
D
hon - ey lov - in', your
hon - ey lov - in' ways.
A7
Yes, I do,
so come to me,
G7
D
yeah. I'll let you be
all my own can - dy, can -
N.C.
D
G/D D
- dy,
my can - dy man.

CARRIE-ANNE

Words and Music by
ALLAN CLARKE, TONY HICKS
and GRAHAM NASH

F/A
G7
C
Dm/A
C
F/A
C
you played a mon - i - tor then you played with old - er boys and pre - fects.
nev - er car - ing, you lost your charm as you were ag - ing.
I'll be your teach - er, when the les - son's o - ver you'll be with me.
Fmaj7/A
G7sus
G7
C
F
G/F♯
What's the at - trac - tion in what they're do - ing.
Where is your mag - ic dis - ap - pear - ing.
Then I'll hear the oth - er peo - ple say - ing.
Hey Car - rie - Anne
G
C
F
G7
what's your game now, can an - y - bod - y play?
C
F
G
C
F
To Coda
Hey Car - rie - Anne what's your game now, can an - y - bod - y

1
G7
2
G7
F
play?
play?
You're so
so
Bb
F
like a wom-an to me
(So like a wom-an to me)
so
Bb
(so)
so
like a wom-an to me.
(Like a wom-an to me.)
G7sus
G7
G7sus
G7
C6
Hey Car-rie - Anne

G C F G7

what's your game now, can a - ny - bod - y play?

C F G/F♯ G C F

Hey Car - rie - Anne what's your game now, can an - y - bod - y

G7

D.S. al Coda

play?

CODA G7

play?

F C/E G7 C

Car - rie - Anne Car - rie - Anne Car - rie - Anne. Car - rie Anne.

CATCH US IF YOU CAN

Words and Music by
DAVE CLARK and
LENNY DAVIDSON

Catch Us If You Can - 2 - 1

F
Dm
F
Now we got-ta run, mm, No more time for fun, mm.
mf
Dm
F
When we're get-tin' an - gry, mm, We will yell with all of our might: Catch Us If You Can,
Gm
Am
F
Dm
Gm
Catch Us If You Can, Catch Us If You Can,
f
Am
Dm
D. S. al ⊕ Coda
Catch Us If You Can.
(snap fingers)
Coda
Dm
F
(snap fingers)
pp

CHAIN OF FOOLS

Words and Music by
DON COVAY

Freely

N.C.

Moderate rock ♩ = 118

mf

Chain, chain, chain,

𝄋 *Chorus:*

Am7

chain, chain, chain,

chain, chain, chain,

Verse:

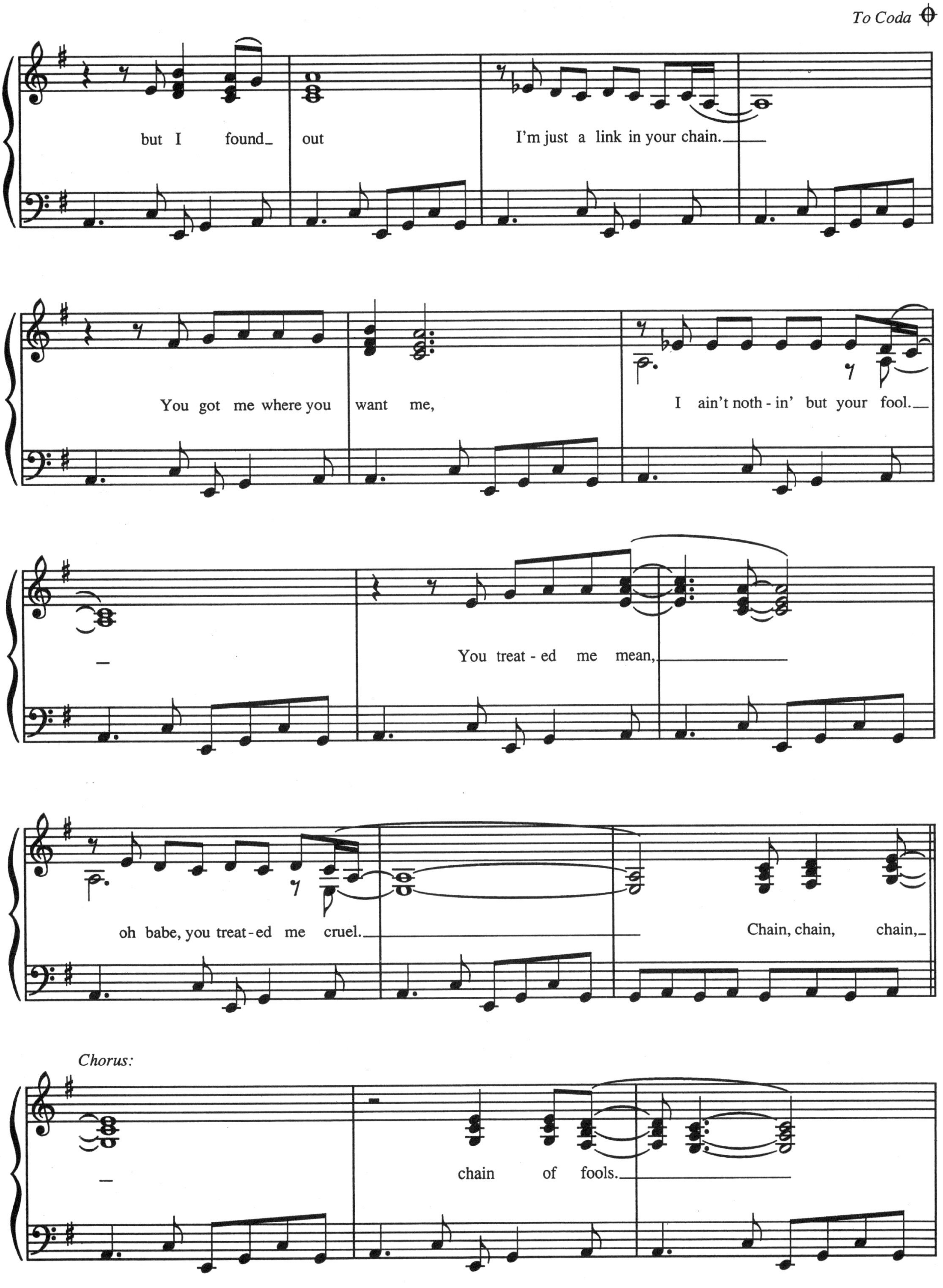

To Coda 𝄌

but I found out I'm just a link in your chain.

You got me where you want me, I ain't noth-in' but your fool.

You treat-ed me mean,

oh babe, you treat-ed me cruel. Chain, chain, chain,

Chorus:

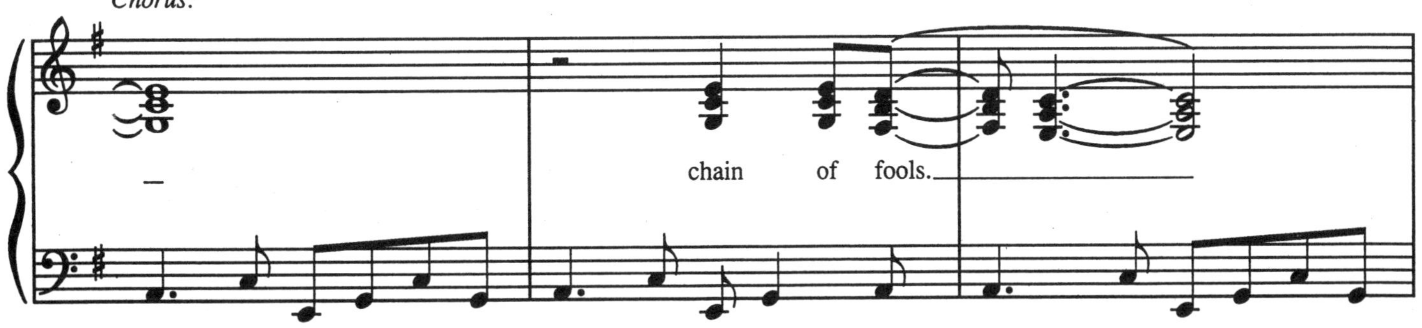

Now, ev - er - y chain
has got a weak
link
I might be weak,
child,
oh, but I gave you strength.
Now, you tell
(hoo, hoo;)
me to leave you a - lone.
My pa - pa says, "Come on home."
(hoo, hoo;)
(hoo, hoo;)
(hoo, hoo;)
My doc - tor says, "Take it eas - y." But your
(hoo, hoo;)
(hoo, hoo;)
(hoo, hoo;)

D.S. 𝄋 al Coda

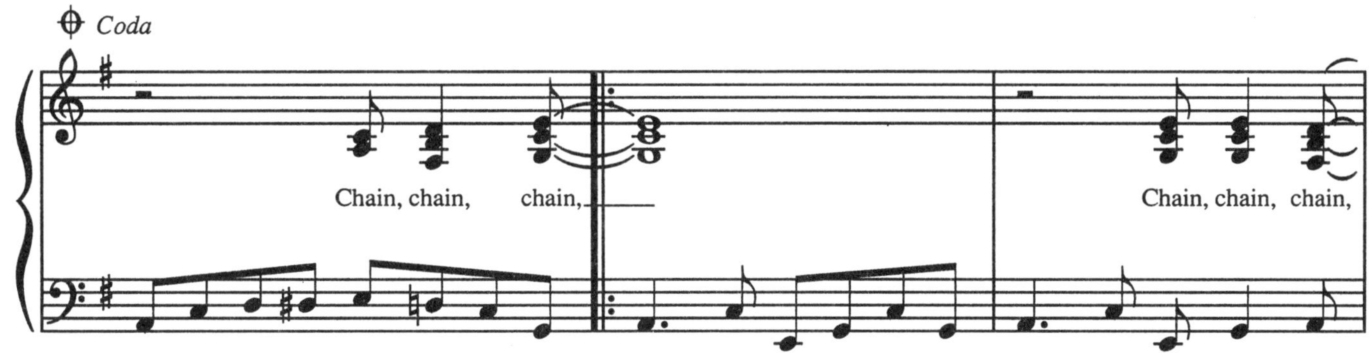

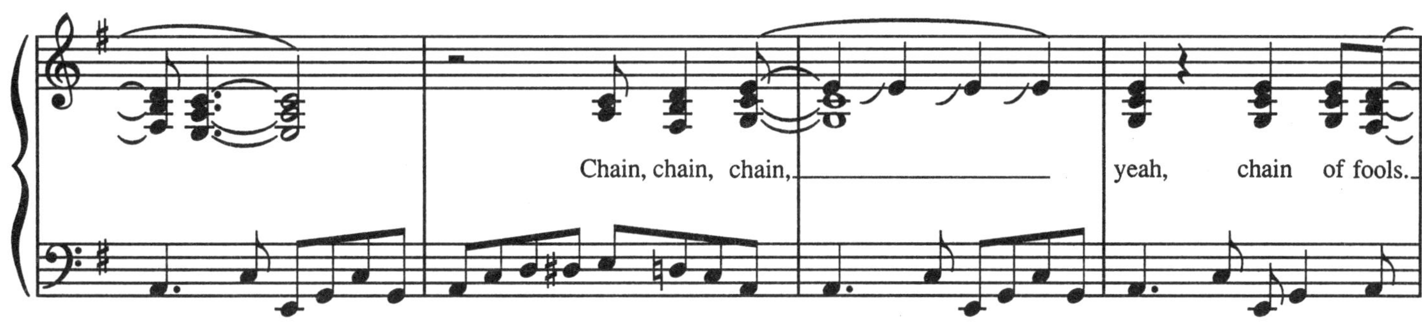

Verse 2:
One of these mornings that chain is gonna break.
But up until then, I'm gonna take all I can take.
(To Coda)

CRYING

Words and Music by
ROY ORBISON and
JOE MELSON

Verse 2:
I thought that I was over you,
But it's true, so true;
I love you even more than I did before.
But darling, what can I do?
For you don't love me and I'll always be
Crying over you, crying over you.
Yes, now you're gone and from this moment on
I'll be crying, crying, crying, crying,
Yeah, crying, crying over you.

CALIFORNIA DREAMIN'

Words and Music by
JOHN PHILLIPS and
MICHELLE PHILLIPS

E7
Am
G
To Coda
F
G
Bm7
Cal - i - for - nia dream-in'
On such a win - ter's day.
Stopped in - to a church,
I passed a - long the way.
F
C
E
Dm6
Oh, I got down on my knees,
And I pre - tend to pray.
You know the preach - er likes the cold,
He knows I'm gon - na stay.
3

E7
Am
G
F
G
Cal - i - for - nia dream - in'
On such a win - ter's
Bm7
E7
D.S. al Coda
day.
All the leaves are
CODA
F
G
On such a win - ter's
Am
G
F
G
Am
G
F
G
day. (Cal - i - for - nia dream - in') On such a win - ter's day. (Cal - i - for - nia dream - in') On such a win - ter's
Fmaj7
Am
day.

DEDICATED TO THE ONE I LOVE

Words and Music by
LOWMAN PAULING and
RALPH BASS

Moderately

D7

While

D9 G Em C

I'm far __ a - way from you __ my ba - by, ____ I

D9 G Em C

know ________ it's hard for you my ba - by, ____ Be -

D9
Em
Bm
Am7
cause ___ it's hard for me my ba - by. ___ And the dark-est hour ___
D7
G
D7
___ is just be - fore dawn.
Each
While
D9
G
D7
night be - fore ___ you go to bed ___
I'm ___ far ___ a - way from you ___
My ba - by ___
D7
G
___ Whis - per a lit - tle ___ prayer for me my

D
D7
D9
To Coda I
ba - by.
(Yeah)
And then tell
Be cause it's
Gdim7
G
all the stars a - bove.
This is de - di -
no chord
To Coda II
ca - ted to the one I love.
Life can nev - er be ex -
act - ly like we want it to be, I could be sat - is -

fied knowing you love me. There's one thing I want you to
do especially for me And it's something that
Am
A7
D9
D7
D.S. al Coda I
ev'rybody needs.
CODA I
Em
Bm
Am7
hard for me my baby, And the darkest hour

D7 G7 Bm Em

— is just be-fore dawn. There's — one thing I want you to

G Bm C Bm no chord E♭

do es-pe-cial-ly for me, and it's some-thing —

D7 D.S. al Coda II

ev-'ry-bod-y needs. —

CODA II

Em Em C

love — This is de-di-ca-ted to the one I love — This is de-di-

DO WAH DIDDY DIDDY

Words and Music by
JEFF BARRY and
ELLIE GREENWICH

D7
fine, (Yeah, yeah) He looked good, he looked fine, and I near-ly lost my mind. Be-
door, (Yeah, yeah) We walked on to my door, and he
mf
D7
G
Em
stayed a lit-tle more. My, my, my, my, I knew we were fall-in' in
more broadly
C
D7
love, My, my, my, my, I told him all the things I was
cresc.
G
C
G
dream-in' of. Now we're to-geth-er near-ly ev-'ry sin-gle day, Sing-in'
mf
f

C
G
DO WAH DID - DY DID - DY, down did - dy do;
We're so hap - py and that's
mf
how we're gon - na stay, Sing - in' DO WAH DID - DY DID - DY, down did - dy do. 'Cause I'm
f
his, (Yeah, yeah) and he's mine, (Yeah, yeah) Well, I'm his and he's mine and the
wed - din' bells will chime, Sing - in' DO WAH DID - DY DID - DY, down did - dy do,
Repeat and Fade

DON'T MAKE ME OVER

Words by
HAL DAVID

Music by
BURT BACHARACH

Bm
F
G7
I would - n't change one thing a - bout you.
now that you know how I a - dore you.
C
Am
Am(G bass)
1. Don't pick on the things I say, the things I do. Just love me with
2. Just take me in - side your arms, and hold me tight and al - ways be
F
G7
all my faults the way that I love you. I'm beg - gin' you.
by my side, if I am wrong or right. I'm beg - gin' you.
3

C
C (E bass)
F
F♯dim7
Don't make me o - ver,
don't make me o - ver,
C (G bass)
Am
F
G
To Coda
now that you've got me at your com - mand.
C
Am
C
Am
D.S. al Coda
no repeat
Ac - cept me for what I am,
ac-cept me for the things that I do.
Coda
C
Am
C
Am
Repeat and fade
Vocal ad lib.
Ac-cept me for what I am,
ac-cept me for the things that I do.

DO YOU KNOW THE WAY TO SAN JOSE

Words by
HAL DAVID

Music by
BURT BACHARACH

Moderately, rhythmically

mf mp

sfz sfz sfz sfz

8va bassa

mf mp

sfz sfz sfz sfz

8va bassa

Excitedly

F Bb6 F

Do you know the way to San_ Jo - se? I've been a- way so
You can real - ly breathe in San_ Jo - se. They've got a lot of

mp

C7(sus) C7 F

long. I_ may go wrong and lose_ my way. Do you know the
space. There'll be a place where I_ can stay. I was born and

R.H.

Bb6
F
C7(sus)
way to San_ Jo - se? I'm go - ing back to find some_ peace of
raised in San_ Jo - se. I'm go - ing back . to find some_ peace of
C7
Am7
Dm7
mind in San_ Jo - se. L. A. is a great_ big free - way.
mind in San_ Jo - se. Fame and for-tune is_ a mag - net.
mf
Am7
Dm7
Am
Put a hun-dred down_ and buy_ a car.
It can pull you far_ a - way_ from home.
F# m7-5
Gm7/F
C/E
In a week may - be two, they'll make you a star.
With a dream in your heart you're nev - er a - lone.

Gm7
C
(Tacet)
Weeks turn in - to years. How quick they pass, and all the stars
Dreams turn in - to dust and blow a - way, and there you are
that nev - er were are park-ing cars and pump - ing gas.
with-out a friend. You pack your car and ride a - way.
mp
1.
2.
F
I've got lots of
mp
sfz
B♭6
Fmaj7
friends in San Jo - se.
mf
mp

F
B♭6
Fmaj7
Do you know the way to San Jo - se?
mf
F
B♭6
Can't wait to get back to San Jo - se.
mp
Fmaj7
Fmaj7
(Tacet)
mf
mp
dim.
poco
8va bassa
Keep repeating and fade
a
poco

DON'T LET THE SUN CATCH YOU CRYING

Words and Music by
GERARD MARSDEN, FRED MARSDEN,
LES CHADWICK and LES MAGUIRE

E7
Am
E7
Em
bro - ken to - night but to - mor-row in the morn - ing light,
Dm7
G7
Cmaj7
Fmaj7
don't let the sun catch you cry - ing.
Cmaj7
Fmaj7
Cmaj7
The night - time
It may be
Fmaj7
Cmaj7
Fmaj7
shad - ows dis - ap - pe - ar
hard to dis - cov - er
3

Cmaj7
Fmaj7
G
and with them go all your tears.
that you've been left for an - oth -
G7
Am
E7
For the morn-ing will bring joy for
er But don't for - get that life's a game and it
Am
E7
Em
Dm7
G7
ev - 'ry girl and boy. So,
al-ways comes a - gain. Oh,
don't let the sun catch you
Cmaj7
To Coda
Fmaj7
Cmaj7
cry - ing.

Fmaj7
F#m7♭5
G
Am
We know that cry-ing's not a bad thing.
Dm
G7
3
But stop your cry-ing when the birds sing.
D.S. al Coda
CODA
Fmaj7
Don't let the
Cmaj7
Fmaj7
Cmaj7
sun catch you cry - ing, oh no, oh oh oh.

DOWNTOWN

Key of G (D-D)

Words and Music by
TONY HATCH

*Chord names and diagrams for guitar.

G
C
D
G
help, I know.
DOWN-TOWN. Just listen to the music of the
never close.
DOWN-TOWN. Just listen to the rhythm of a
☆ And you may find somebody kind to
f
Em
G
Em
traffic in the city. Linger on the sidewalk where the neon signs are pretty.
gentle Bossa Nova. You'll be dancing with 'em too before the night is over,
help and understand you. Someone who is just like you and needs a gentle hand to
Bm
C
How can you lose?
happy again.
guide them along.
1} The lights are much brighter there, you can for-
2}
(3) So, maybe I'll see you there, we can for-
mf
mp
Em7
A
Em7
A
G
Gmaj.7
get all your troubles, forget all your cares. So go DOWN-TOWN,
get all our troubles, forget all our cares. So go DOWN-TOWN,
f

Am7
D6
D9
G
Gmaj.
things-'ll be great when you're DOWN - TOWN.
where all the lights are bright DOWN - TOWN,
things-'ll be great when you're DOWN - TOWN.
No fin - er place, for sure,
wait - ing for you to - night
Don't wait a min - ute more
ff
Gmaj.7
DOWN - TOWN.
Ev - 'ry - thing's wait - ing for you
You're gon - na be al - right now
Ev - 'ry - thing's wait - ing for
fff
1.2.
3.
DOWN - TOWN.
you
mf
DOWN - TOWN.
DOWN - TOWN.
Repeat and fade

FERRY 'CROSS THE MERSEY

Words and Music by
GERARD MARSDEN

With a beat

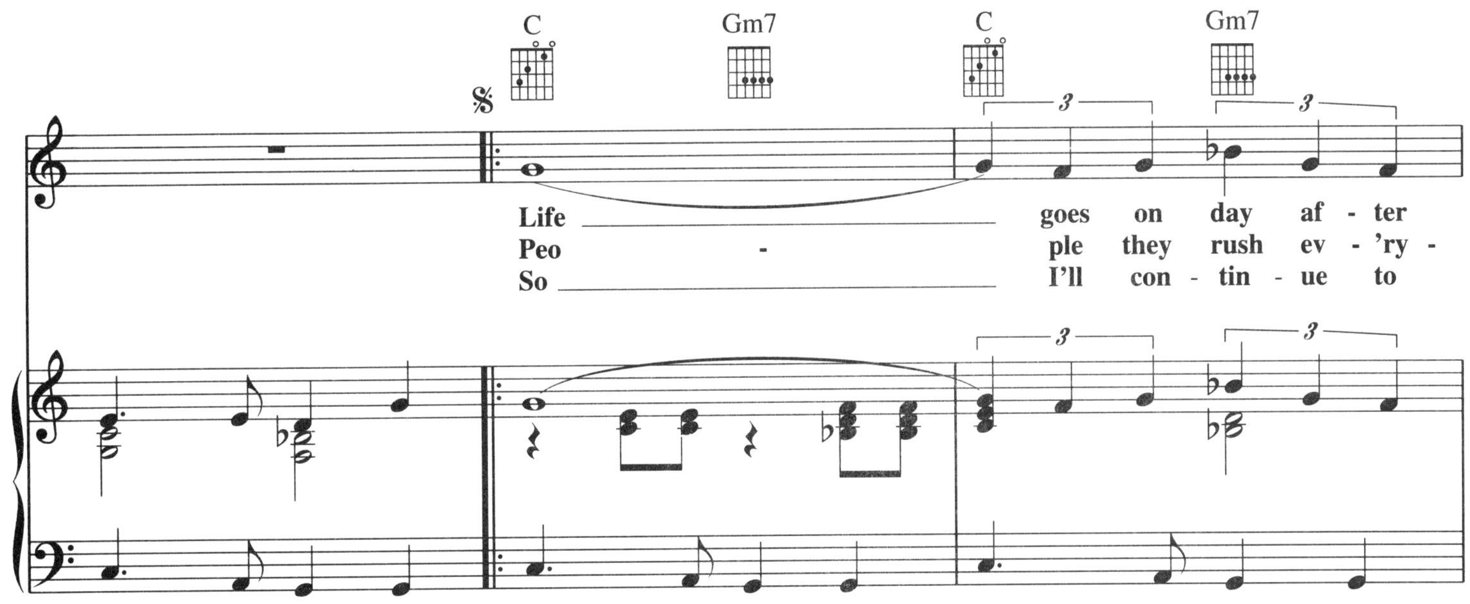

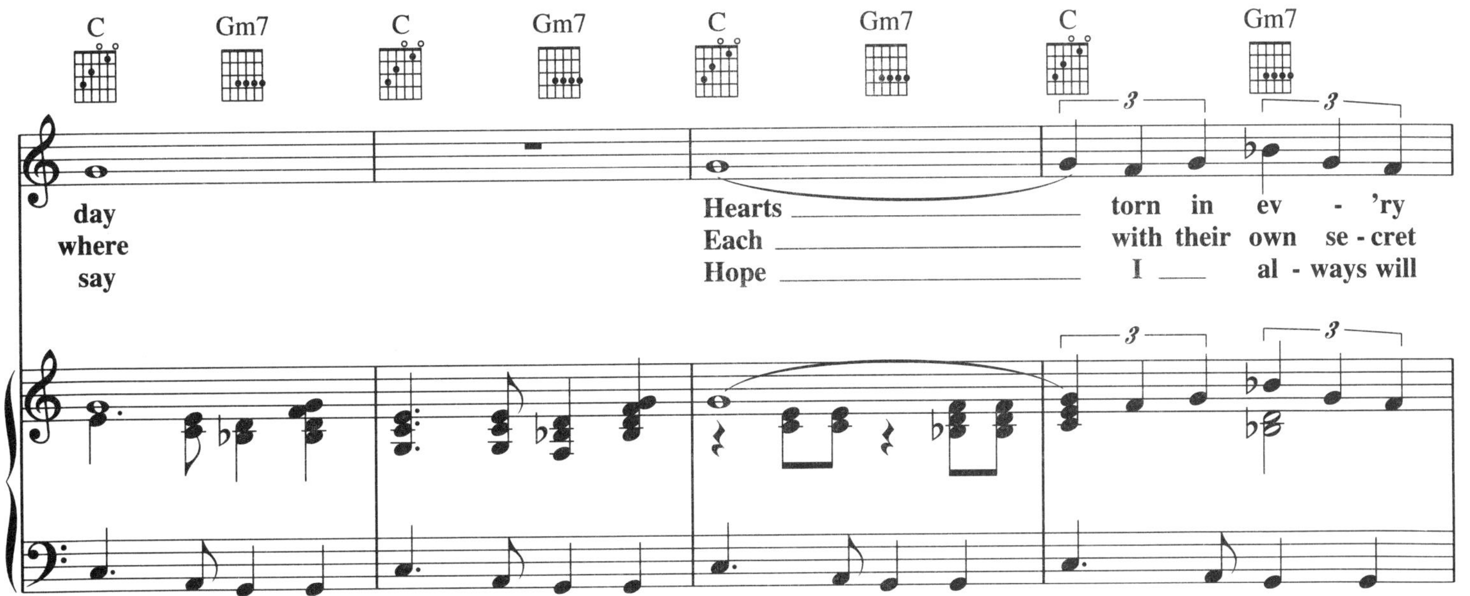

C
Gm7
C
Gm7
G7
C
way
care
stay
So fer - ry cross the
So fer - ry cross the
So fer - ry cross the
Em
Dm
G7
To Coda
Mer - sey 'Cos this land's the place I love And here I'll
Mer - sey And al - ways take me there The place I
Mer - sey 'Cos this land's the place I love And here I'll
1
C
Gm7
C
Gm7
2
C
stay
love
3
3
Dm
G7
C
Peo - ple a - round ev - 'ry cor - ner

Dm
G7
C
Dm
G7
They seem to smile and say
We don't care what your
Em
D7
G7
D.S. al Coda
name is boy
We'll nev - er send you a - way
CODA
C
Gm7
C
Gm7
C
Gm7
stay
And here I'll stay
C
Gm7
C
Gm7
C
Gm7
C
Here I'll stay.

GEORGY GIRL

Words by
JIM DALE

Music by
TOM SPRINGFIELD

Eb
Gm
Ab
Bb
Eb
Gm
1. Why do all the boys just pass you by? Could it be you just don't
2. Dream-ing of the some - one you could be. Life is a re - al - i -
Ab
Db
Bb7(sus 4)
Bb7
Bb9
Cm
try, or is it the clothes you wear? You're al-ways
ty, you can't al-ways run a - way. Don't be so
Gm
Ab
Eb
win - dow shop - ping but nev - er stop - ping to buy.
scared of chang - ing and re - ar - rang - ing your - self.
G
C
F
Bb
Bb7
So shed those dow - dy feath - ers and fly a lit - tle bit.
It's time for jump-ing down from the shelf

Eb Gm Ab Bb Eb Gm Ab Bb
Hey there! Geor-gy girl, There's an-oth-er Geor-gy deep in - side.
Eb Gm Ab Bb7 Cm
Bring out all the love you hide and oh, what a change there'd be,
Cm7 Ebmaj7 Ab Bb7 1. Eb Gm
The world would see A new Geor-gy girl.
Ab Bb7 2. Eb Repeat ad lib. and fade Gm Ab Bb7
girl. A new Geor-gy

GIMMIE SOME LOVIN'

Words and Music by
STEVE WINWOOD, MUFF WINWOOD
and SPENCER DAVIS

E A/E E A/E E A/E
want-ing some more. Let me in, ba - by. I don't know what you've got. But you'd
place is on fire. Been a hard day__ and I don't know what to do.
place is on fire. Been a hard day,__ noth - in' went too good. Now I'm
E A/E E A/E E G
bet - ter take it eas - y. This__ place is hot.
Wait a min - ute, ba - by. It could hap - pen to you.
gon - na re - lax, hon - ey. Ev - 'ry - bod - y should.__
So glad__ we made__
A C
__ it, so glad__ we made__ it. You got - ta
E A/E E A/E
To Coda
gim - me some lov - in', gim - me some lov - in',

E
A/E
E
gim - me some lov - in' ev - er - y day.
D/E
A/E
D/E
A/E
E7
Hey!
3
E
A/E
1.
E
A/E
2.
E
A/E
D.S. al Coda
Well, I
Well, I
Repeat and fade
Coda
E
A/E
E
A/E
gim - me some lov - in',
gim - me some lov - in',

GO WHERE YOU WANNA GO

Words and Music by
JOHN PHILLIPS

G
C
G
C
G
do what you wan-na do with whom - ev- er you wan-na do it, babe.
G
D
Em
C
You don't un - der - stand that a girl like me can love
D
just one man.
G
F
Em
Three thou - sand miles, that's how far you'll
You've been gone a week and I've tried so

D
Em
To Coda
A7
D7
G
go,
hard
And you said to me
Not to be the cry
Please
Em
D
don't go.
You've got - ta
G
C
go where you wan-na go,
do what you wan-na do with whom-ev - er you wan - na do
no chord
it, babe. You've got-ta go where you wan-na go,
do what you wan-na do with

G
C
G
D.S. al Coda
whom-ev - er you wan-na do___ it!
CODA
A7
D7
- in' kind,_
G
Em
A
Not to be ___ the girl you left be - hind. ___
3
D
G
C
Go where you wan-na go,_
G
C
G
C
G
Repeat and Fade
do what you wan - na do__ with whom-ev - er you wan - na do___ it.

GOIN' OUT OF MY HEAD

Words and Music by
TEDDY RANDAZZO and
BOBBY WEINSTEIN

Slowly with a beat

2.
Cmaj7
Dm7/G G7
Cmaj7
Dm7
-ist. Go - in' out of my head o - ver you, out of my
Cmaj7
Dm7
C F6 C F6 C F6
head o - ver you, out of my head day and night, night and day and
C F6 C
D
Fm6
night wrong or right. I must think of a way in - to your
C
Cdim
G G7 F♯dim/G
heart. There's no rea - son why my be - ing shy should keep us a -
G
Cm7
Cmaj7
Repeat and fade
dim.
part. And I think I'm go - ing out of my head. Yes I

HELLO MARY LOU

Words and Music by
GENE PITNEY and
CAYET MANGIARACINA

Edim Bb Gm Cm7 F7-9 Bb
to the ground, And though I nev - er did meet you be - fore.
good an' tight, That's all I had to see for me to stay.
Eb Bb F7 Bb7 Eb
I said "hel - lo Ma - ry Lou good - bye
Bb C9 Am C7 F7
heart Sweet Ma - ry Lou I'm so in love with you.
Bb F9 Bb D7 D+ D7 Gm C9 C7
knew Ma - ry Lou We'd nev - er part so hel - lo Ma - ry
F7 Dm F7 Bb F7 Bb
Lou good - bye heart." I heart."

HE'S A REBEL

Words and Music by
GENE PITNEY

*Sing vocal one octave lower.

2.
G7
C
C♯7
guy.
just be-cause of that they say . . .
Chorus:
F♯
D♯m
F♯
f
He's a reb-el and he'll nev-er, ev-er be an-y good.
He's a reb-el 'cause he
C♯7
B
nev-er, ev-er does what he should. Well, just be-cause he does-n't do what
A♯
D♯m
ev-'ry-bod-y else does, a-that's no rea-son why

B
G♯7
F♯
(2nd time only:)
I can't give him all my love.
we can't share our love.
He is al - ways good to me,
D♯m
B
(3rd time only:)
al - ways treats me ten - der - ly,
good to him I'll try to be.
'cause he's not a reb - el, oh, no, no,
C♯7
To Coda
F♯
C♯7
he's not a reb-el, no, no, no, to me.
Solo:
F♯
D♯m
F♯

D♯m
B
C♯7
B
C♯7
D♯m
If they don't like him that way, they
B
G♯7
C♯7
D.S. 𝄋 al Coda
won't like me af - ter to - day, and I'll be stand-ing right by his side when they say . . .
3
3

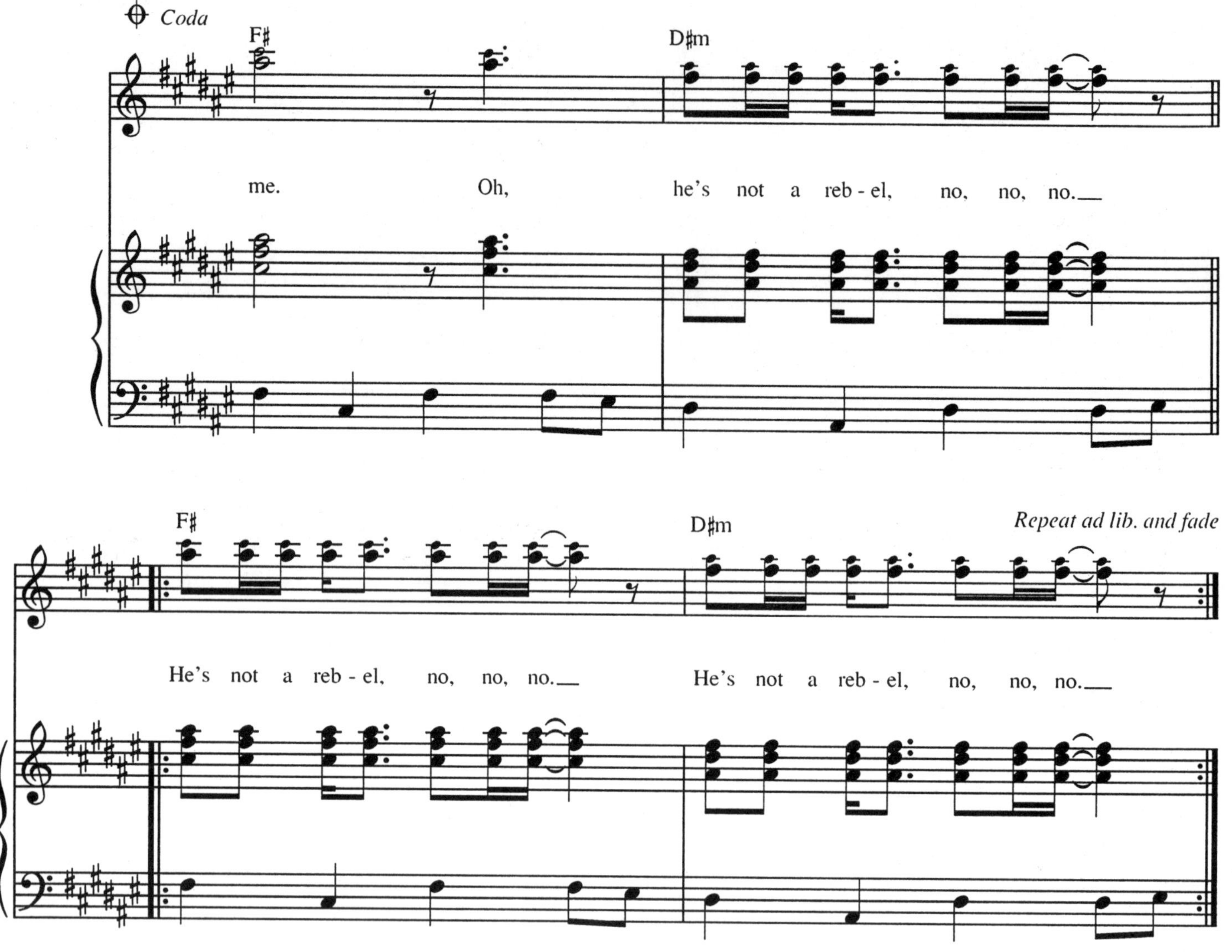

Verse 2:
When he holds my hand, I'm so proud,
'Cause he's not just one of the crowd.
My baby's always the one to try the thing they've never done,
And just because of that they say . . .
(To Chorus:)

THE HOUSE OF THE RISING SUN

Words and Music by
ALAN PRICE

Verses 2 & 3
Dm F G B♭ Dm F A7
moth - er was a tai-lor ___ Sewed my new blue jeans My
on - ly thing a gambler needs Is a suit - case and a trunk And the
Dm F G B♭ Dm A7 Dm F
fa - ther was a gam - blin' man Down in New Or - leans.
on - ly time he'll be sat-is-fied Is when he's all a - drunk.
G B♭ Dm A7
1. Dm A7
3. Now the
2. Dm A7
Verse 4
Dm F G B♭ Dm F
4. Oh! moth-er, tell your chil-dren ___ Not to do what I have
A7 Dm G B♭ Dm A7
done Spend your lives ___ in sin and mis-er-y ___ In the house ___ of the Ris - ing

Dm F G B♭ F A7
Sun.
Dm A7 Verses 5 & 6 Dm F G B♭
5. Well I've got one foot on the plat-form The
is a house in New Or - leans They
Dm F A7 Dm F
oth - er foot on the train I'm go - ing back to
call the Ris - ing Sun And it's been the ruin of
G B♭ Dm A7 Dm F
New Or - leans To wear that ball and chain.
ma - ny a poor boy, And God, I know I'm one.
G B♭ Dm A7 1. Dm A7 2. Dm
6. Well there

HOW DO YOU DO IT?

Words and Music by
MITCH MURRAY

Bb
C7
F
Dm7
Gm7
C7
F
give me a feel-ing in my heart
Like an ar-row
pass-ing thro' it
Bb
C7
F
Dm7
G7
C
G9
C
G7
S'pose that you think you're ve-ry smart
But won't you tell me
How do you do it
C7
F
Dm7
Gm7
C7
F
Dm7
Gm7
C7
How do you do what you do to me
If I on-ly knew
Then per-
F
Dm7
Gm7
C7
F
Bb
F
Eb
E
F
Bb
F
Bb
F
1.
2.
haps you'd fall for me like I fell for you.
you.

I GOT YOU BABE

Words and Music by
SONNY BONO

F
Bb
Eb
3fr.
C
Gm7
C7
you got me, and ba - by, I got you,
babe,
I got you, babe.
I got
you, babe.
They say our love won't pay the rent, Be -
fore it's earned our mon - ey's all been spent.
I

F
Bb
F
Eb
3fr.
guess that's so, we don't have a pot, But at least I'm sure of all the things we
C
Gm7
3fr.
C7
F
Bb
got, babe, I got
F
Bb
F
you, babe I got you, babe. I got
Gm
3fr.
Gm7
3fr.
C7
C7
Gm7
3fr.
C7
flow - ers in the Spring, I got

Gm
3fr.
Gm7
3fr.
C7
C7
Gm7
3fr.
C7
F
you, to wear my ring, And when I'm
F
Gm7
3fr.
sad, you're a clown, And if I get
F
C7
C#7
scared you're al-ways a - round. So
F#
B
F#
E
Let them say your hair's too long, 'cause I don't care, with you I can't do

C#
G#m7
4fr.
C#7
F#
B
wrong.
Then put your little hand in mine,
F#
E
C#
G#m7
4fr.
C#7
There ain't no hill or moun - tain we can't climb,
Repeat and fade
F#
B
F#
B
babe,
I got
you, babe.
I got

I ONLY WANT TO BE WITH YOU

Words and Music by
MIKE HAWKER and
IVOR RAYMONDE

1.
2.
I on-ly want to be with you. It
I on-ly want to be with you.
D7 D C D Am7 D7 G C D G C G
You stopped and smiled at me, Asked if I'd care to dance.
Eb G C G
I fell in-to your op-en arms and I did-n't stand a chance.
D Bm7 Em7 A7
Now listen honey, I just wanna be beside you ev-ry-where. As long as were to-gether honey
D7 G Em G

I don't care 'Cos you start-ed somethin' Oh can't you see that
Em C D Am7 D7
ev-er since we met you've had a hold on me. No mat-ter what you do,
G Em Am Bm Am C♯dim.
To Coda
D 𝄋 al
I on-ly want to be with you.
D7 D C D Am7 D7 G C G
Coda.
I said I on-ly want to be with you.
rall.
G C G Am7 D7 G C G

I SAY A LITTLE PRAYER

Words by
HAL DAVID

Music by
BURT BACHARACH

Gm7
Cm7
While comb - ing my hair now and won - d'ring what
At work I just take time and all through my
R.H.
F
B♭
Am7(no 5)
dress to wear now I say a lit - tle prayer for you.
cof - fee break time I say a lit - tle prayer for you.
D7
Excitedly
E♭
F/E♭
Dm7
For - ev - er, for - ev - er you'll stay in my heart and
B♭
A♭/B♭
B♭
B♭9
E♭
Dm7
I will love you for - ev - er and ev - er. We nev - er will part. Oh,
8va

A♭
B♭
B♭9
B♭
E♭
Dm7
how I'll love you. To - geth-er, to-geth - er, that's how it must be. To
B♭
A♭
B♭
B♭9
E♭
F/E♭
1. Smoothly
D
(Tacet)
live with - out you would on-ly mean heart-break for me.
mf
2. Smoothly
D
(Tacet)
Gm7
Cm7
me. My dar - ling, be - lieve me,
mf
p
R.H.
E♭/F
for me there is no one but
mp

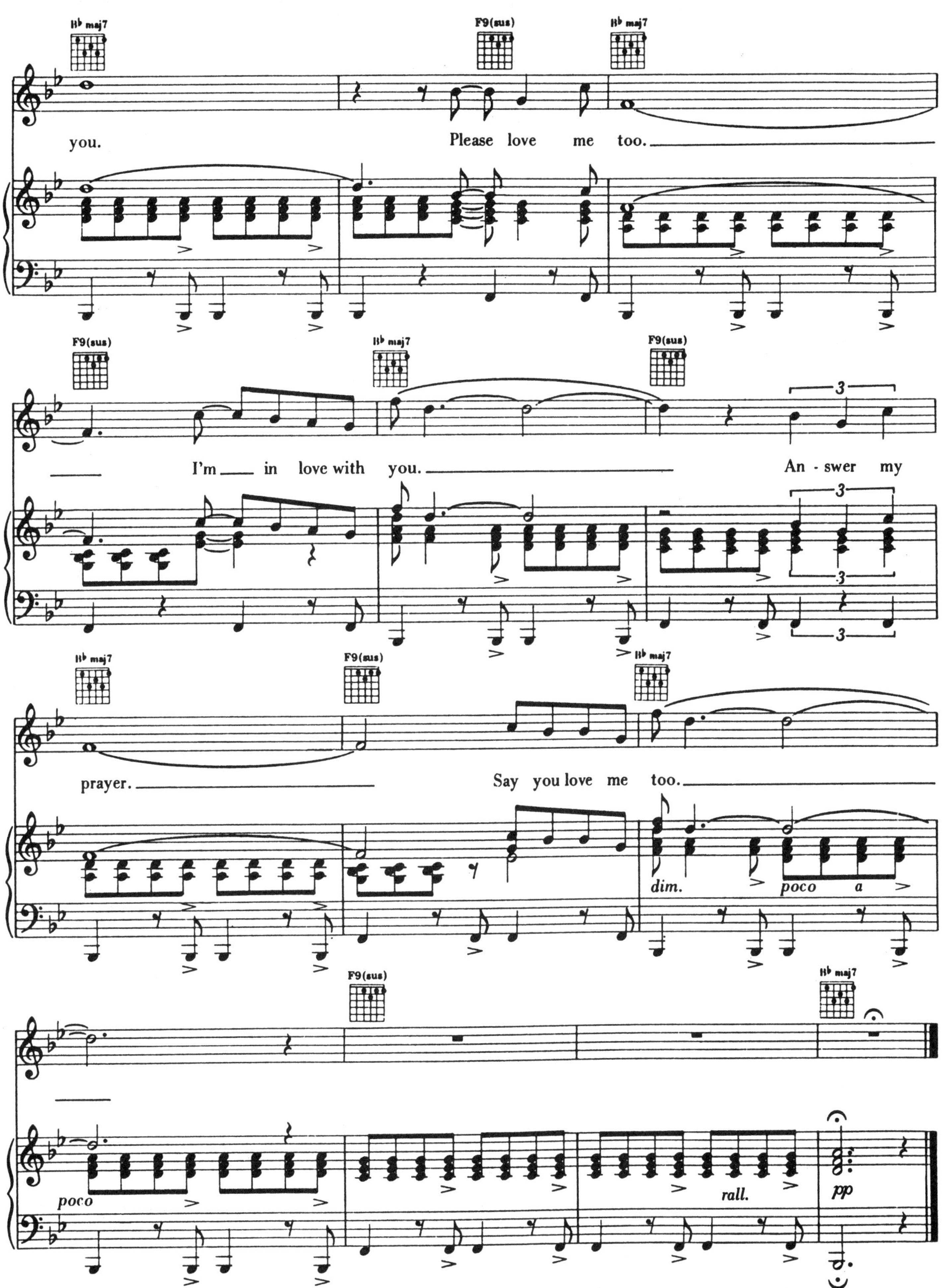
B♭maj7
F9(sus)
B♭maj7
you.
Please love me too.
F9(sus)
B♭maj7
F9(sus)
I'm in love with you.
An - swer my
B♭maj7
F9(sus)
B♭maj7
prayer.
Say you love me too.
dim.
poco a
F9(sus)
B♭maj7
poco
rall.
pp

I WANT TO HOLD YOUR HAND

Words and Music by
JOHN LENNON and
PAUL McCARTNEY

Em
Bm
C
D
I want to hold your hand,
you'll let me hold your hand,
I want to hold your
Now let me hold your
G
Em
C
D
1 G
hand,
hand,
I want to hold your hand.
I want to hold your
Oh,
2 G
Dm7
G
hand.
And when I touch you I feel
more smoothly
C
Am
Dm7
hap - py in - side.
It's such a

G
C
D
C
D
feel - ing that my love I can't hide, I can't hide,
C
D
I can't hide!
G
D
Yeah, you got that some - thing
Yeah, you got that some - thing
as before
Em
Bm
G
I think you'll un - der - stand. When I say that
I think you'll un - der - stand. When I feel that

D
Em
Bm
some - thing,
some - thing,
I want to hold your hand,
C
D
G
Em
1 C
D
I want to hold your hand,
I want to hold your
G
2 C
D
B7
hand.
I want to hold your hand,
C
D
C
G
I want to hold your hand.

IT'S MY PARTY

Words and Music by
HERB WIENER, JOHN GLUCK
and WALLY GOLD

Moderately bright

f

C
D7
G7
hold - ing her hand, when he's sup - posed to be mine?
danc - ing with me, I've got no, rea - son to smile.
birth - day sur - prise, Ju - dy's wear - ing his ring.
C
C+
F
It's my par - ty, and I'll cry if I want to, Cry if I want to,
f
Fm
C
G7
Cry if I want to, You would cry, too, if it hap - pened to
C
F
1,2
G7
3
C
you.

I SAW HER AGAIN LAST NIGHT

Words and Music by
JOHN PHILLIPS and
DENNIS DOHERTY

A
A7
D
G
A
G
just not right. If I could-n't, I would-
I said, though I nev-er think of
F#7
B
B7
n't.
her.
But what can I do?
I'm lone-ly, too,
E
A
C#7/G#
F#m
Bm7♭5/F
and it makes me feel so good to know
she'll nev-er
1
A
E7sus
2
A
leave me.
I'm in way- o-
leave me.

A♭
Ev - 'ry time I see that girl, you
B♭m
G♭
know I want to lay down and die.
But I real - ly
A♭
C♭
need that girl,
though I'm liv - ing a lie.
E♭m
It makes me wan - na

A♭m
C♭
To Coda
cry.
E7sus
A7
I saw her a - gain last night,
D
G
A
C♯m/G♯
and you know that I should - n't
F♯m
E
A
A7
To string her a - long's just not right.

D
G
A
G7
If I could - n't I would -
F#7
B7
E
n't. But what can I do? I'm lone - ly, too, and it makes me
A
C#7/G#
F#m
Bm7♭5/F
A
feel so good to know she'll nev - er leave me.
E
A
A7
D
G

A
C#m/G#
F#m
E
A
A7
D
G
A
G
F#7
But what can I do?
B7
E
E7
I'm lone - ly, too.
Yeah, and it makes me
A
C#7/G#
F#m
Bm7♭5/F
A
feel so good to know she'll nev - er leave me.

D.S. al Coda
CODA
E7sus
I saw her.
A
A7
D
G
I saw her a - gain last night, and you know that I should-
just not right. If I could - n't I would-
ver my head. Now she thinks that I love
I said, though I nev - er think of
A
C#m/G#
F#m
E
Repeat and Fade
n't. To string her a - long's
n't. I'm in way o -
her be - cause that's what
her. I saw her a - gain

MRS. BROWN YOU'VE GOT A LOVELY DAUGHTER

Words and Music by
TREVOR PEACOCK

C
G7
G7
Bb7
ain't no good to pine.
pine.
E
Gm
Ab
Bb
Walk - in' a - bout,
E - ven in a crowd, well,
Gb
Bbm
Bb
G7
You'd pick 'er out,
Made a bloke feel so proud.
C
Em7
Dm7
G7
C
Em7
Dm7
G7
If she finds that I've been 'round to see you,

C
Em7
Dm7
G7
Tell her that I'm well and feel - in' fine;
Am
Don't let on,
Don't say she's broke my heart,
Em
I'd go down on my knees, but it's no good to pine.
Mis - sis Brown you've got a love - ly daugh - ter.
Repeat and Fade

LET IT BE ME

English Words by MANN CUTIS
French Words by PIERRE DELANOE

Music by
GILBERT BECAUD

Gm7 C7♭9 F B♭ Am B♭
let it be me. Each time we meet, love, I find com-
let it be me. To you I'm pray - ing; hear what I'm
F Gm7 F/A B♭ A
plete love. With - out your sweet love, what would life be?
say - ing. Please let your heart beat for me, just me.
F C7/E C7 C♯dim Dm Am/C
So nev - er leave me lone - ly; tell me you'll love me on - ly,
And nev - er leave me lone - ly; tell me you'll love me on - ly,
B♭ F/A Gm7 Gm7/C C7♭9
1. F Gm7 C7
2. F
and that you'll al - ways let it be me. me.
and that you'll al - ways let it be

LET'S TWIST AGAIN

Words and Music by
DAVE APPELL and
KAL MANN

C7
F
C
Ee - ah 'roun' 'n a 'roun' 'n a up 'n down we go a -
F
F♯
G7
gain. Oh ba - by, make me know you love me so, an'
C
Am
then let's twist a - gain, like we did last sum - mer.
F
G
C
Yeah, let's twist a - gain, like we did last year.

THE LION SLEEPS TONIGHT

Lyrics and Revised Music by
GEORGE DAVID WEISS, HUGO PERETTI
and LUIGI CREATORE

B♭
F
C7
ooh wim - o - weh.
wim - o - weh, o - wim - o - weh, o - wim - o - weh, o - wim - o - weh, o - wim - o - weh, o - wim - o - weh.
F
B♭
F
C7
3. F
(Obbligato)
B♭
F
Whuh,
whuh,
whuh wim - o - weh.
Wim - o - weh, o - wim - o - weh, o - wim - o - weh, o - wim - o - weh, o - wim - o - weh, o - wim - o - weh, o -
mf
C7
F
B♭
Wee
wim - o - weh, o - wim - o - weh, o - wim - o - weh, o - wim - o - weh, o - wim - o - weh, o - wim - o - weh, o -
F
C7
F
ooh wim - o - weh.
Wee
wim - o - weh, o - wim - o - weh, o - wim - o - weh, o - wim - o - weh.
p-pp
B♭
F
1.
2.
ooh wim - o - weh.

LOVE IS ALL AROUND

Words and Music by
REG PRESLEY

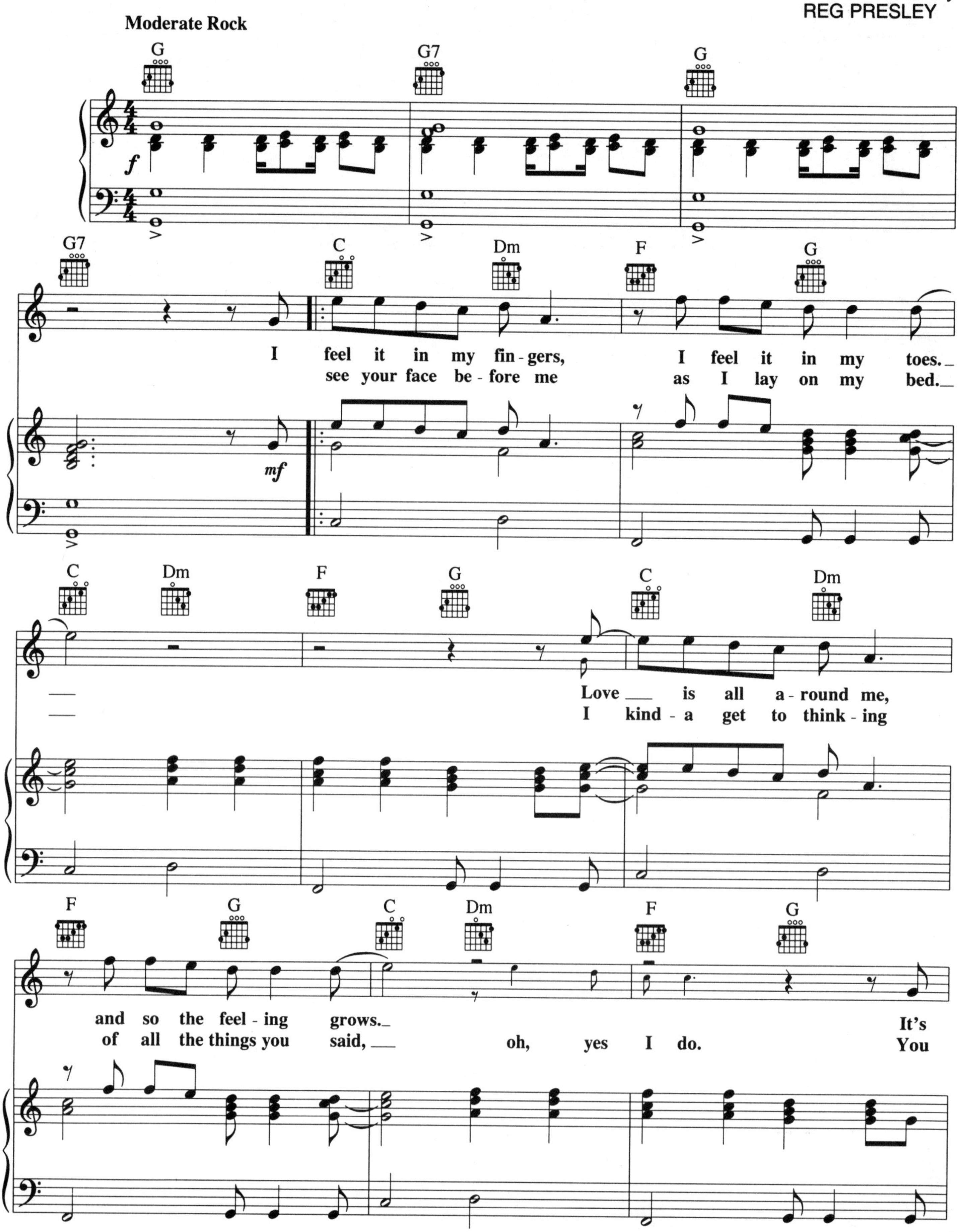

Moderate Rock

G G7 G

G7 C Dm F G

I feel it in my fin - gers, I feel it in my toes. _
see your face be - fore me as I lay on my bed. _

C Dm F G C Dm

Love _ is all a - round me,
I kind - a get to think - ing

F G C Dm F G

and so the feel - ing grows. _ It's
of all the things you said, _ oh, yes I do. You

C Dm F G C Dm
writ-ten on the wind, it's ev-'ry-where I go, oh, yes it is.
give your prom-ise to me and I give mine to you.
F G C Dm F G
So if you real-ly love me, come on and let it show,
I need some-one be-side me in ev-'ry-thing I do,
C Dm F G
N.C.
oh.
oh, yes I do.
F Dm F
You know I love you, I al-ways will. My mind's made up by the

C F Dm

way that I feel. There's no be - gin - ning, there'll be no end, 'cause

1 G

on my love you can de - pend.

C Dm F Gsus C Dm

F Gsus 2 G Gsus G Gsus

I can de - pend.

G
Gsus
G
C
Dm
Got-ta keep it mov - ing.
Ooh, it's writ-ten in the wind, oh,
F
G
C
Dm
F
G
ev-'ry-where I go.
So
C
Dm
F
G
C
Dm
if you real - ly love me, love me, love me,
come on and let it show.
F
G
C
Dm
F
G
Repeat and Fade
Come on and let it show.
Come on and let it show.

MAKE IT EASY ON YOURSELF

Words by
HAL DAVID

Music by
BURT BACHARACH

C
E♭
E♭ aug
don't try to spare my feel-ings,
just tell me that we're

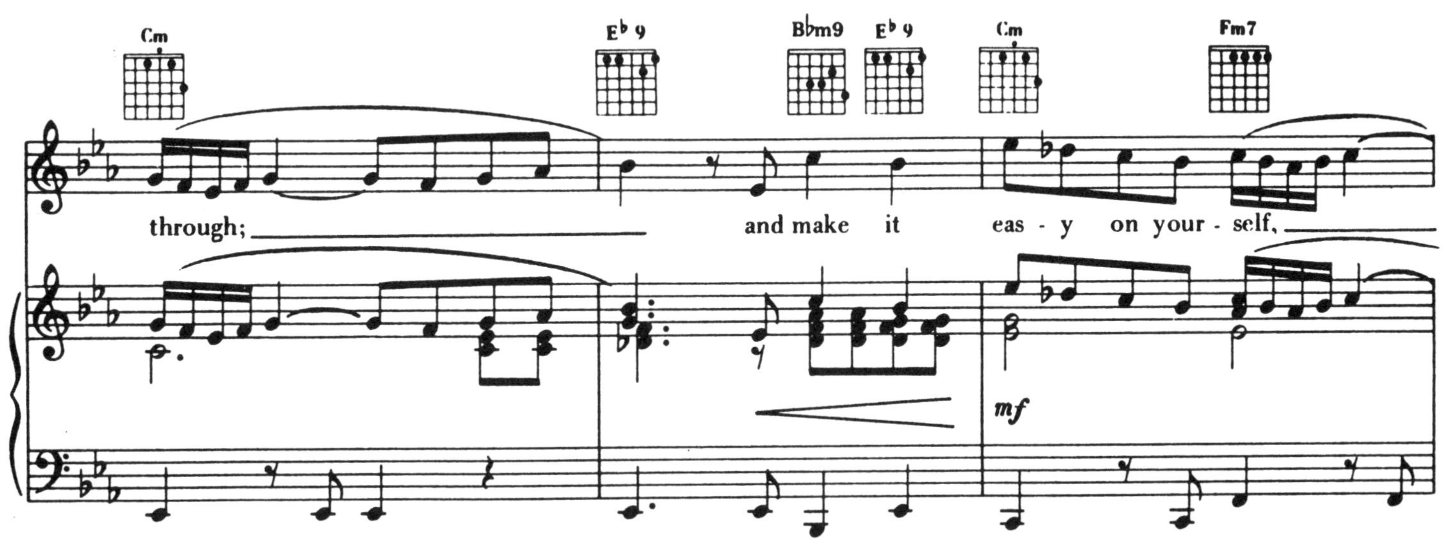

Cm
E♭ 9
B♭m9
E♭ 9
Cm
Fm7
through;
and make it
eas - y on your - self,
mf

D♭
E♭ 9
Cm
Fm7
D♭
E♭
make it
eas - y on your - self
'cause

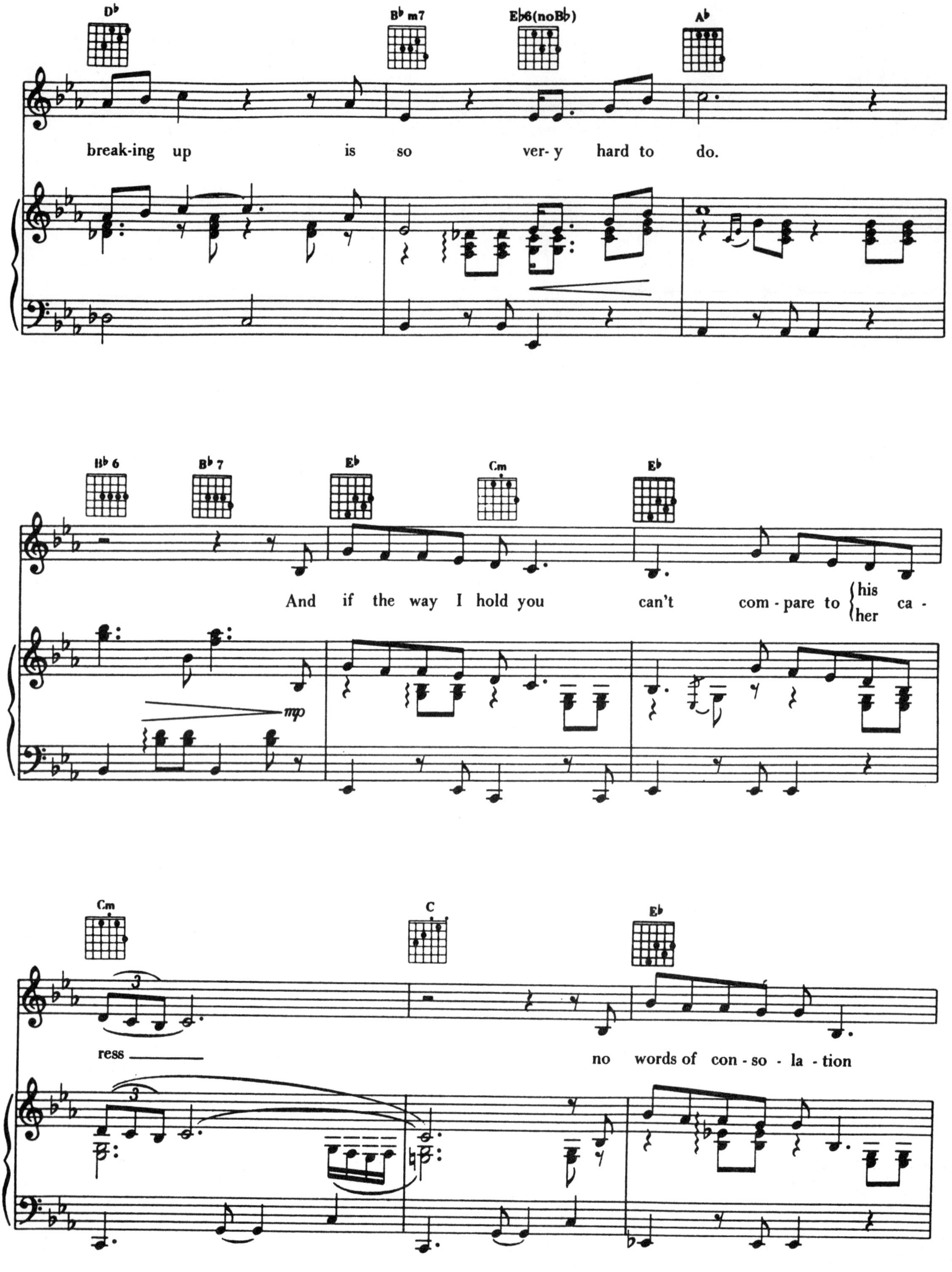

D♭ B♭m7 E♭6(noB♭) A♭

breaking up is so very hard to do.

B♭6 B♭7 E♭ Cm E♭

And if the way I hold you can't compare to {his / her} ca-

E♭ aug
Cm
E♭9
B♭m9
E♭9
will make me miss you less. My dar - ling,
Cm
Fm7
D♭
E♭9
Cm
Fm7
if this is good - bye, I just know I'm gon - na cry
mf
D♭
E♭
D♭
B♭m7
E♭6(noB♭)
so, run to {him {her be - fore you start cry - in'
A♭
A♭6
B♭m9
E♭9
Cm
Fm7
too; And make it eas - y on your - self,
mf

D♭
E♭9
Cm
Fm7
D♭
E♭
make it eas - y on your - self
'cause
D♭
B♭m7
E♭6(no B♭)
A♭
break-ing up is so ver - y hard to do. Oo
Cm
D♭
E♭6(no B♭)
A♭maj7
Whoa-o-o - o oh oh.
dim. poco a poco
rall.
ppp

MESSAGE TO MICHAEL

Words by
HAL DAVID

Music by
BURT BACHARACH

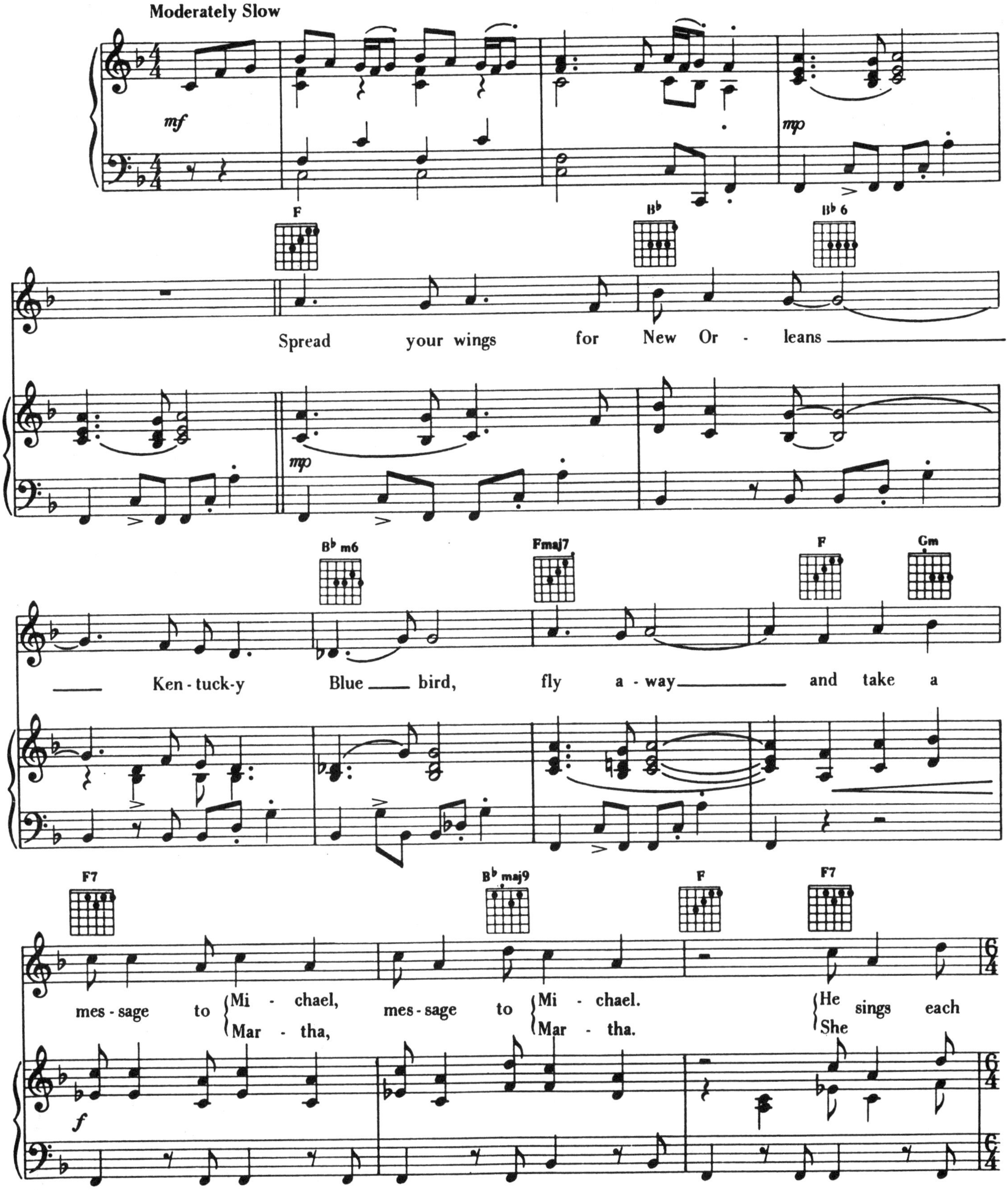

Moderately Slow

mf

mp

F Bb Bb6

Spread your wings for New Or - leans

Bb m6 Fmaj7 F Gm

Ken - tuck-y Blue bird, fly a - way and take a

F7 Bb maj9 F F7

mes - sage to {Mi - chael, / Mar - tha,} mes - sage to {Mi - chael. / Mar - tha.} {He / She} sings each

f

B♭maj7
B♭
B♭6
B♭m
F
B♭
night in some ca - fe. In {his / her} search to find wealth and fame.
mp
C
C9
C7
F
B♭6
I hear {Mi - chael / Mar - tha} has gone and changed {his / her} name.
mf
3
F
B♭
B♭6
It's a year since {he / she} was here Ken - tuck - y
mp
B♭m6
Fmaj7
F
Gm
F7
Blue - bird, fly a - way and take a mes - sage to {Mi - chael, / Mar - tha,}
f

B♭maj9
F
F7
B♭maj7
B♭
B♭6
B♭m
mes - sage to {Mi - chael. / Mar - tha.} Tell {him / her} I miss {him / her} more each day. As {his / her}
F
B♭
C
train pulled out down the track, {Mi - chael / Mar - tha} pro - mised {he'd / she'd}
mp
C9
C7
F
C
Tacet
soon be com - ing back. Oh, tell {him / her} how my heart just breaks in
mf
Am
F
Tacet
two, since {he / she} jour - neyed far, And e - ven though {his / her} dream of

C
Am
B♭
B♭ maj7
fame fell through, to me {he / she} will al - ways
C
F
B♭
B♭ 6
be a star.
Spread your wings for New Or - leans
Ken-tuck-y
mp
B♭ m6
Fmaj7
F
Gm
Blue - bird, fly a - way and take a
F7
B♭ maj9
F
F7
mes-sage to {Mi - chael, / Mar - tha,} mes-sage to {Mi - chael. / Mar - tha.} Ask {him / her} to
f

B♭maj7
B♭
B♭6
B♭m
F
B♭
start for home to - day. When you find {him, / her,} please let {him / her} know
mp
C
C9
C7
F
B♭
B♭6
Rich or poor, I will al - ways love {him / her} so.
mf
mp
F
B♭
B♭6
F
Fly a - way, Ken - tuck - y Blue - bird, fly a - way, Ken -
mf
B♭
F
Keep repeating and fade out
tuck - y Blue - bird. Fly a - way, fly a - way.
dim. poco a poco

NEVER MY LOVE

Words and Music by
DICK and DON ADDRISI

C
E7sus4
E7
Am7
D9
mf
What makes you think love will end When you
How can you think love will end When I've
Gmaj7
Cmaj9
Fmaj7
Dm7
know that my whole life de - pends on
asked you to spend your whole life with
Em
Am
C
G
you?
me?
Slower
a tempo
mp
You say you fear I'll change my mind
Bb
F
C
Am
C
I won't re-quire you,
Nev-er My Love,
F
C
D. S. al Coda
Nev-er My Love.
Coda
Am9
dying out
8va
ppp
Ped.

ONLY THE LONELY
(Know The Way I Feel)

Words and Music by
ROY ORBISON and
JOE MELSON

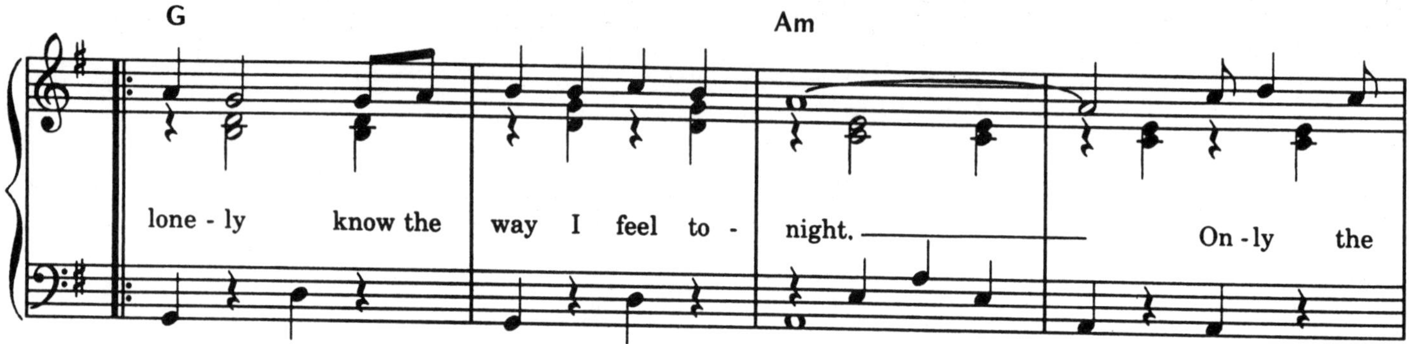

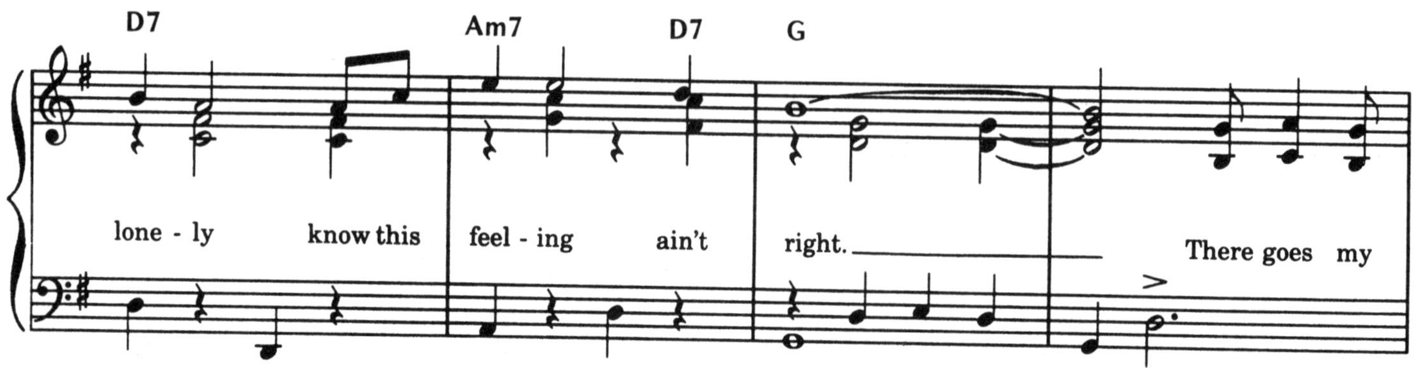

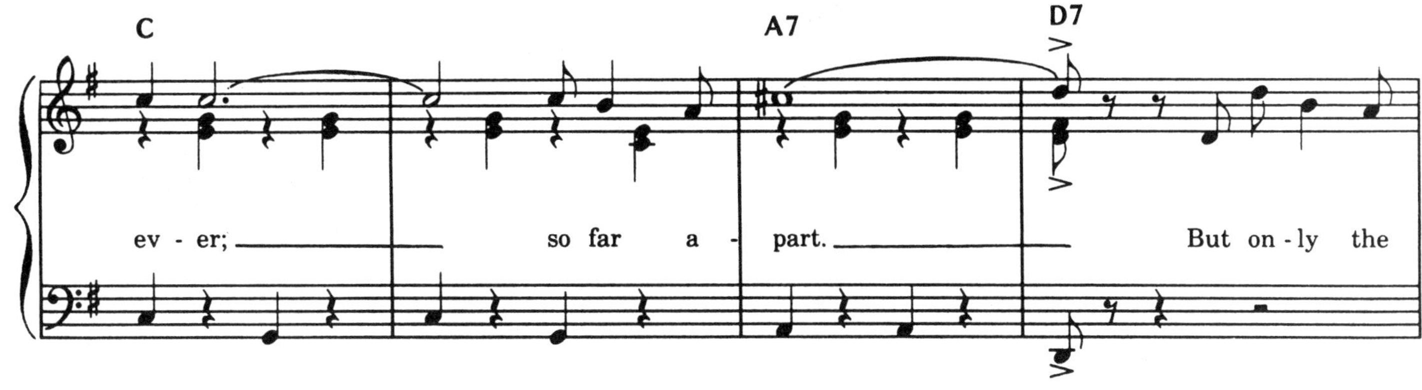

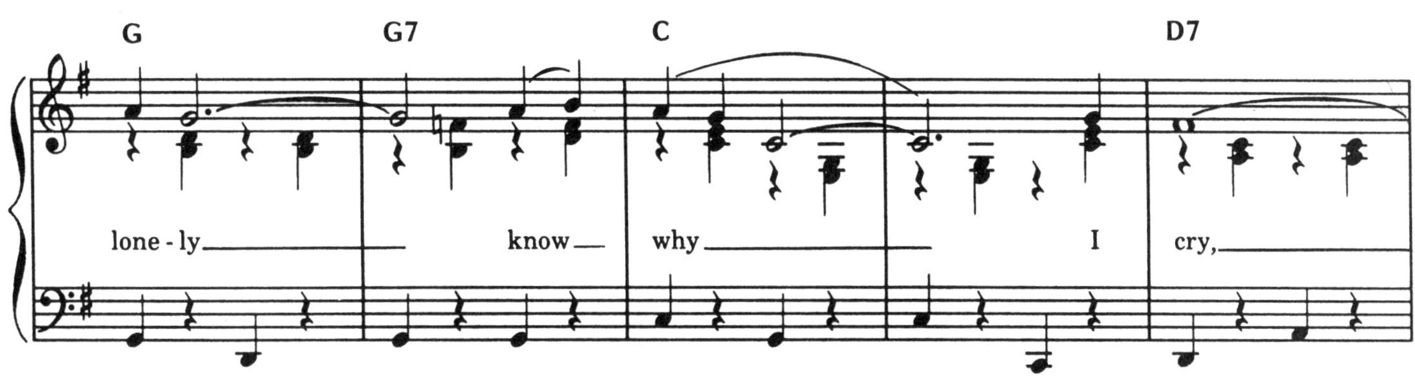

Verse 2:
Only the lonely know the heartaches I've been through.
Only the lonely know I cry and cry for you.
Maybe tomorrow, a new romance;
No more sorrow, but that's the chance
You've got to take if you're lonely.
Heartbreak, only the lonely.

ONLY LOVE CAN BREAK A HEART

Words by
HAL DAVID

Music by
BURT BACHARACH

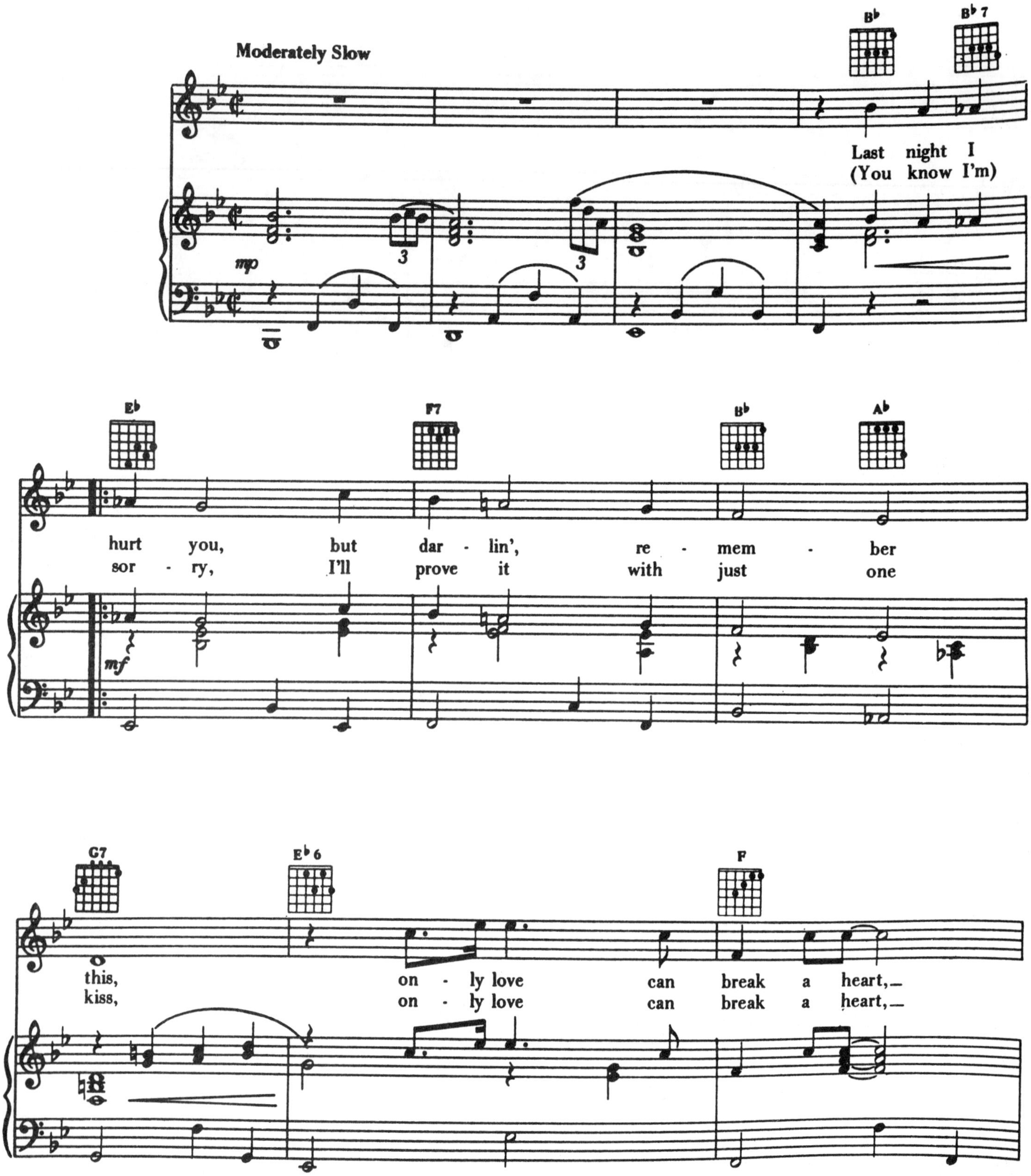
Moderately Slow
B♭
B♭7
Last night I
(You know I'm)
mp
E♭
F7
B♭
A♭
hurt you, but dar - lin', re - mem - ber
sor - ry, I'll prove it with just one
mf
G7
E♭6
F
this, on - ly love can break a heart,—
kiss, on - ly love can break a heart,—

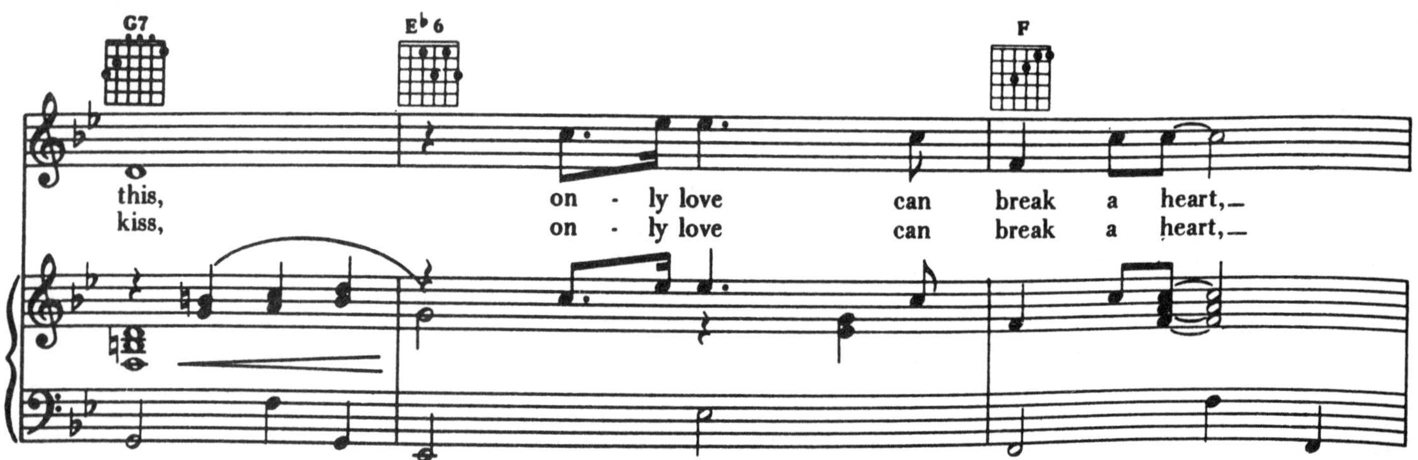

1.
2.
E♭6
F
B♭
B♭7
F7
E♭
Cm
C7
only love can mend it a gain.
You know I'm gain.
Give me a
chance to make up for the harm I've
done, try to for - give me and let's keep the

F7
E♭
F7
tacet
two of us one!
Please let me
mf
E♭
F7
B♭
hold you and love you for al - ways and
G7
E♭6
F
al - ways,
on - ly love can break a heart,
E♭6
F
F7
B♭
E♭
B♭
on - ly love can mend it a - gain.
rall.

PLEASE, PLEASE ME

Words and Music by
JOHN LENNON and
PAUL McCARTNEY

C D7 G 1 D7 2 G

Yeh like I please you.

C D7 G

I don't want to sound com - plain - ing But you know there's al - ways rain in my ______ heart.

C D7

I do all the pleas - ing with you It's so hard to rea - son with

G C D7 G

you. Oh yeh why do you make me blue.

G
B♭ C D7
3
Last night I said these words to my girl,
G
C
I know you nev - er e - ven try girl Come on, come
Am Em C G C D7
on, come on, come on Please please me oh yeh like I please
1 G D7
2 G
you.
you.

REACH OUT FOR ME

Words by
HAL DAVID

Music by
BURT BACHARACH

C
Am
Dm7
They make you feel that your heart will just nev - er stop
They make you feel that you have - n't a rea - son for
G6
G
Am
ach - in'. And when you just can't ac -
liv - in'. So when you feel you could
Dm7
G6
G
cept the a - buse you are tak - in'. Dar - lin',
throw in the towel and just give in,
Gm7
C6
Gm9
reach out for me, Don't you wor - ry, I'll see you through.

C6
Gm9
C6
You just have to reach out for me,
I'll be there and
Gm9
C6
B♭6
Am7
I'll com - fort you, Oh, yes, I will. Com-fort you and love you,
B♭maj7
C7
oh, How I'm gon - na love you.
La la la la la
F
Dm
C7
Repeat - ad lib. - fading out
La, La la la la la, La la la la la

RUNNING SCARED

Words and Music by
ROY ORBISON and
JOE MELSON

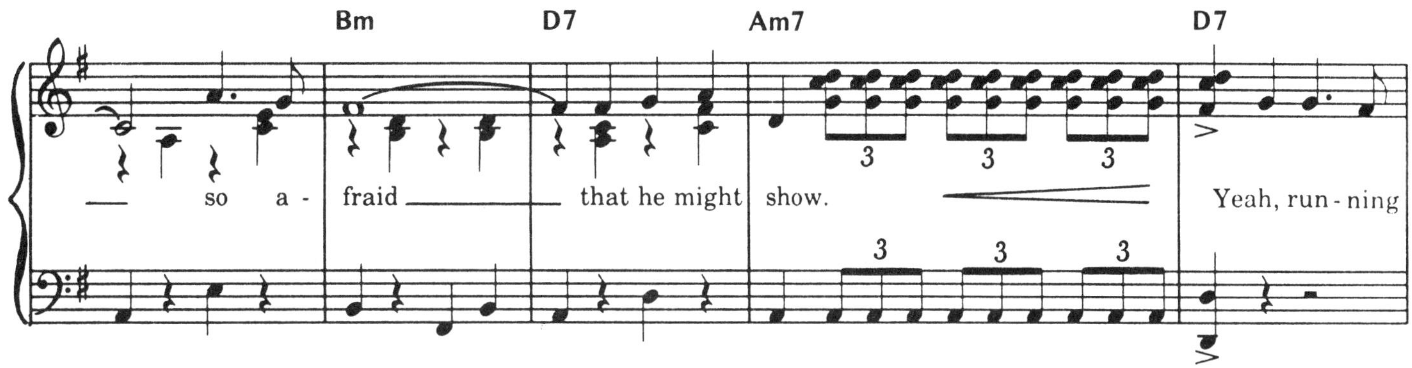

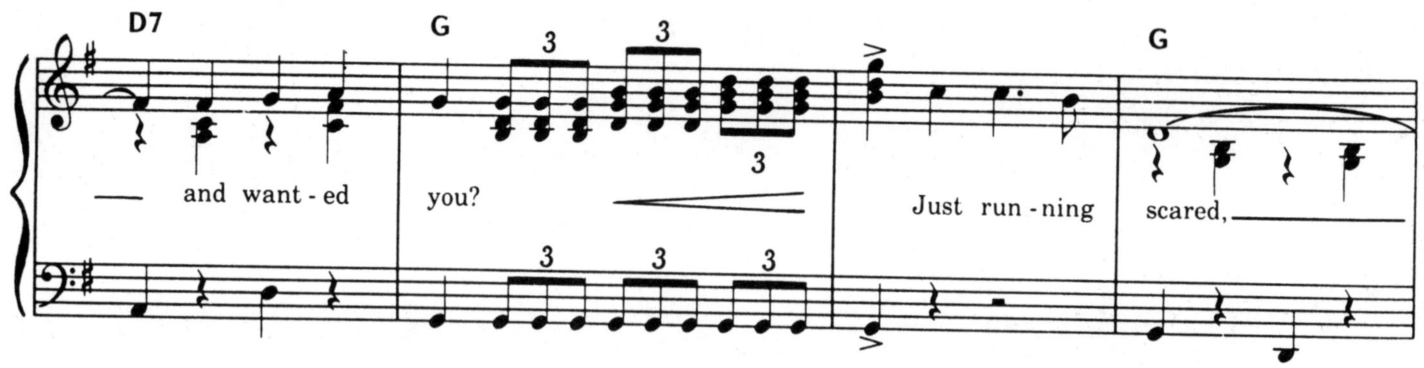
D7
G
G
3
3
3
— and want - ed
you?
Just run - ning
scared, ___
3
3
3

Am
Bm
— feel - ing
low. ___
Run - ning
scared, ___
you loved him

D7
G
so. ___
Just run - ning
scared, ___
a - fraid to

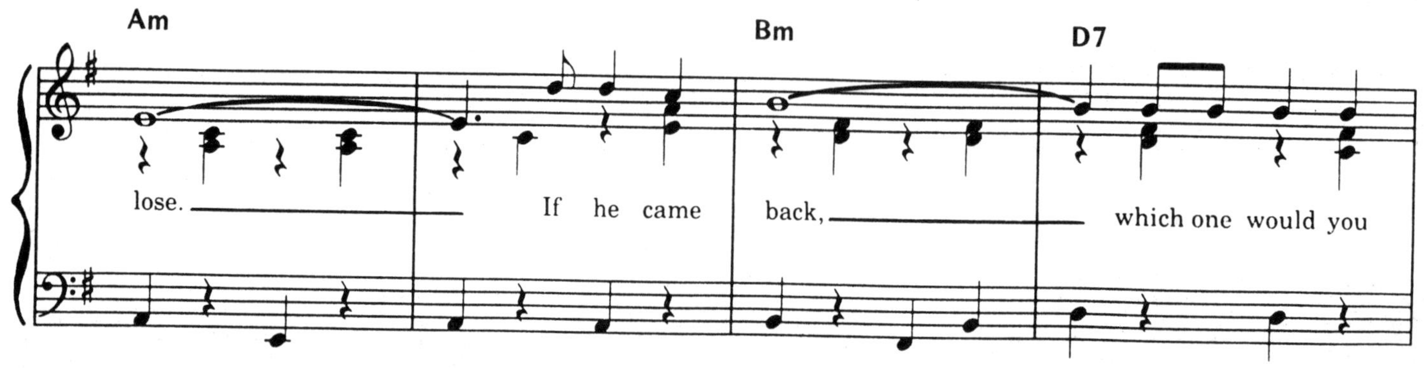
Am
Bm
D7
lose. ___
If he came
back, ___
which one would you

G
G7
C
choose?
Then all at once,
he was stand-ing there,

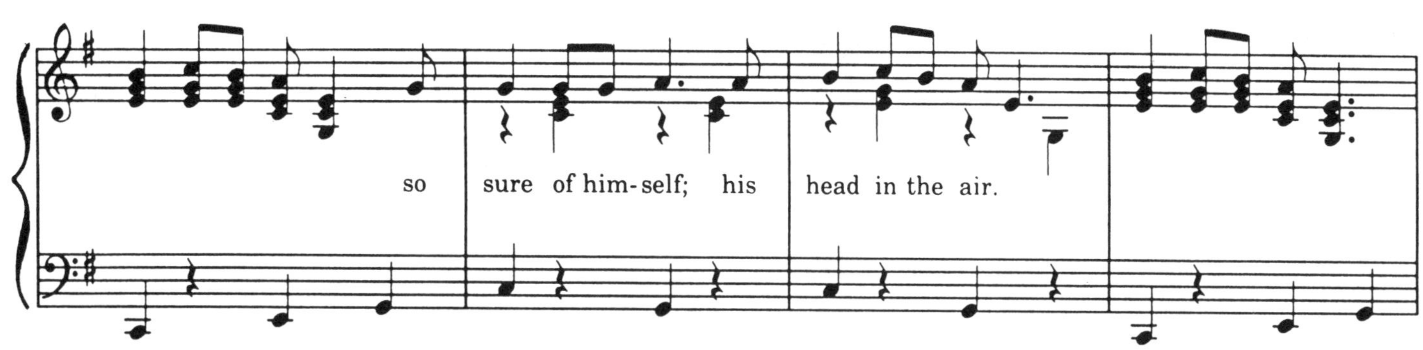
so
sure of him-self; his
head in the air.

D7
My heart was break-ing; which
one would it be?
You turned a-round and
walked a-way with

1.
2.
G
G
me.
Just run-ning
me.
ff

RUNAROUND SUE

Words and Music by
DION DI MUCCI and
ERNIE MARESCA

2.
A
D
hayp. Ah
I should have known it from the ve - ry start,
I miss her lips and the smile on her face, the
Bm
G
this girl will leave me with a bro - ken heart.
touch of her hair and this girl's warm em - brace.
Now lis - ten peo - ple what I'm
So if you don't wan - na cry
A
N.C.
tell - ing you
like I do
a - keep a - way from a Run - a - round Sue.
D
Bm
Hayp hayp bum - da ha - dy ha - dy, hayp hayp bum - da ha - dy ha - dy,
(Oh, oh, oh, oh,

G
A
hayp hayp bum-da ha-dy ha-dy hayp. Ah
oh, oh.)
G
D
She likes to trav-el a-round,
she'll love you but she'll put you down.
G
A
N.C.
Now peo-ple let me put you wise,
Sue goes
D
out with oth-er guys. Here's the mor-al and the sto-ry from the guy who knows,

Bm
G
I fell in love and my love still grows.
Ask an - y fool that
A
N.C.
D
she ev - er knew they'll say keep a - way from - a Run - a - round Sue.
Hayp hayp
Bm
(Fade after D.S.)
bum - da ha - dy ha - dy, hayp hayp bum - da ha - dy ha - dy,
G
A
N.C.
D.S. al fade
hayp hayp bum - da ha - dy ha - dy hayp. Ah

THE WANDERER

Words and Music by
ERNEST MARESCA

1. C
2. C
To next strain
round.
2. Well now, there's
round.
Oh well, I
3. C
Fine
G7
round.
roam from town to town,
I go thru
life with - out a care;
And I'm as hap - py as a clown
With my
A7
D7
G7
D. S. al Fine
two fists of i - ron and my bot - tle of beer.
3. Oh well,

RUNNING BEAR

Words and Music by
J. P. RICHARDSON

Eb
F7
Bb
F7
her name such a love - ly sight to see. But their
see her throw - ing kiss - es 'cross the waves. Her lit - tle
lips met the rag - ing ri - ver pulled them down. Now they'll
Bb
F7
Bb
Bb/F
F7
tribes fought with each oth - er, so their love could ne - ver
heart was beat - ing fas - ter wait - ing there for her
always be geth - er in that hap - py hunt - ing
Bb
Bb7
Eb
Bb
be.
brave. Run - ning Bear loved lit - tle White Dove with a
ground.
F7
Bb
Bb7
Eb
Bb
love big as the sky. Run - ning Bear loved lit - tle White Dove with a
F7
1 Bb
F7
2 Bb
F7
3 Bb
love that could - n't die He could - n't die. Run - ning die.

SECRET AGENT MAN

Words and Music by
P. F. SLOAN and
STEVE BARRI

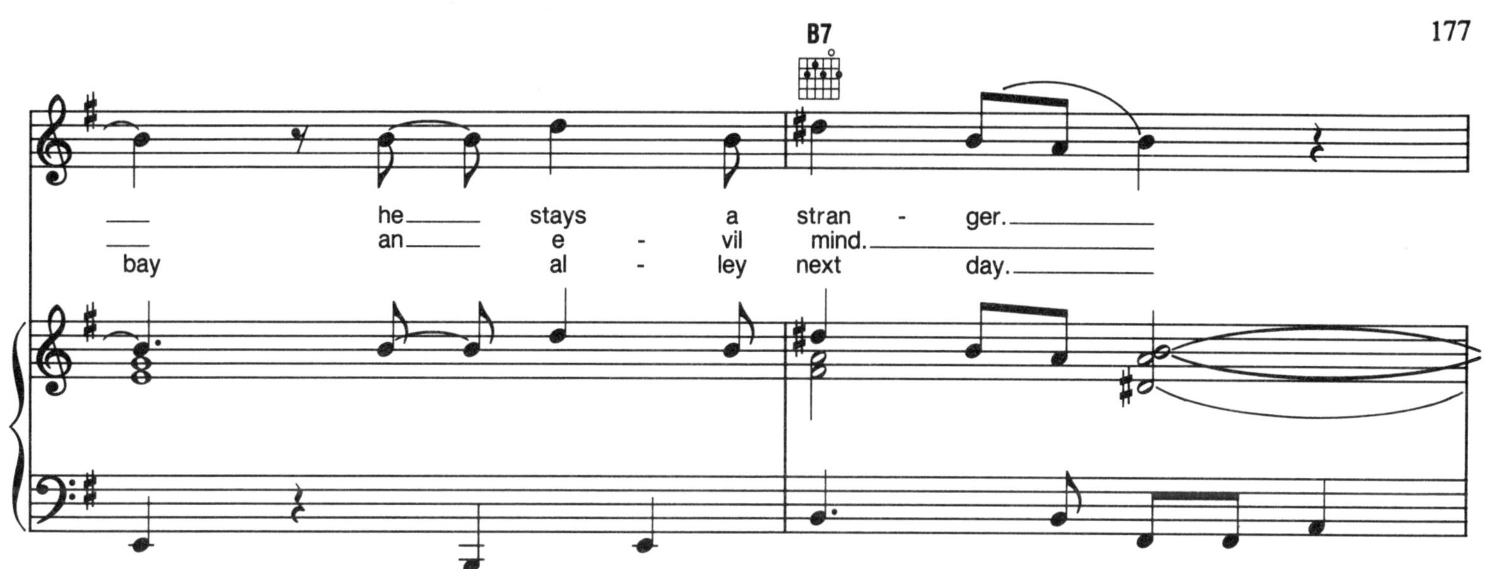
B7
he stays a stran - ger.
an e - vil mind.
bay al - ley next day.

Em
Oh With ev - 'ry move he makes
be care - ful what you say.
Oh, no, you let the wrong word slip

Am
an - oth - er chance he takes.
You'll give your - self a - way.
while kiss - ing per - sua - sive lips.
The

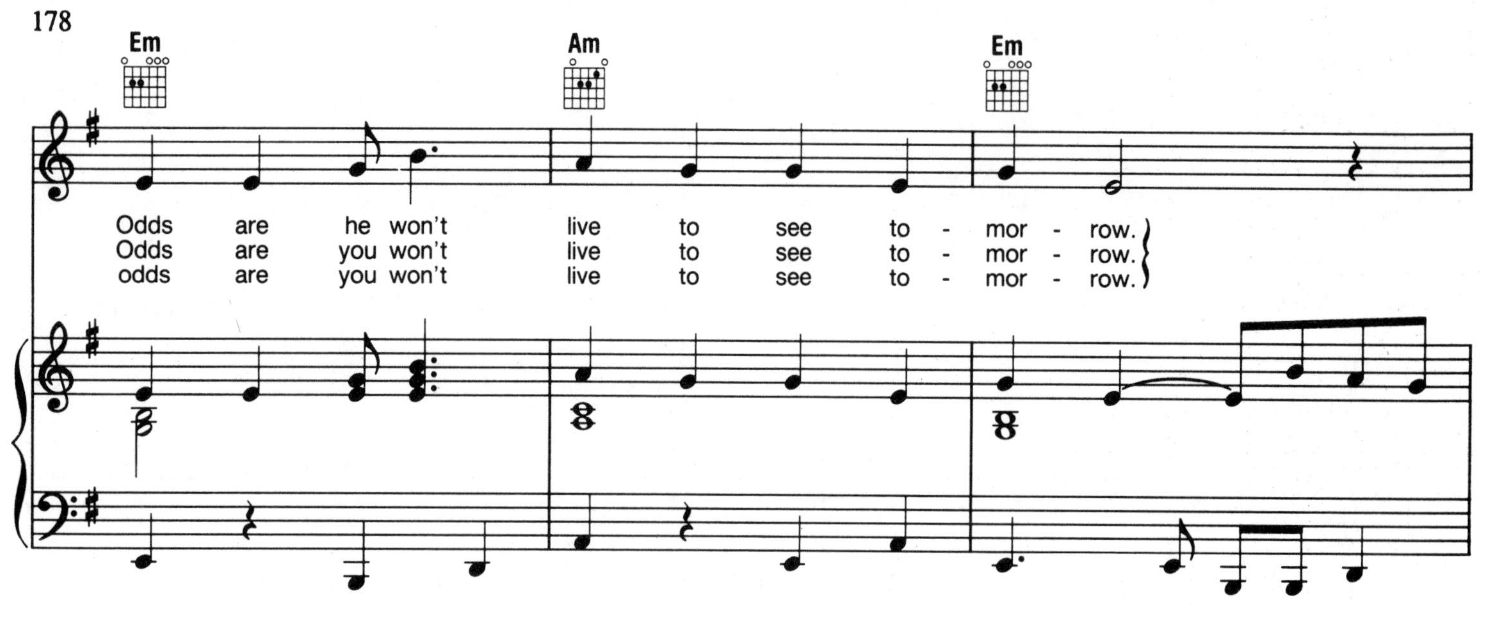
Em
Am
Em
Odds are he won't live to see to - mor - row.
Odds are you won't live to see to - mor - row.
odds are you won't live to see to - mor - row.

Bm
Em
Se - cret a - gent man, se - cret

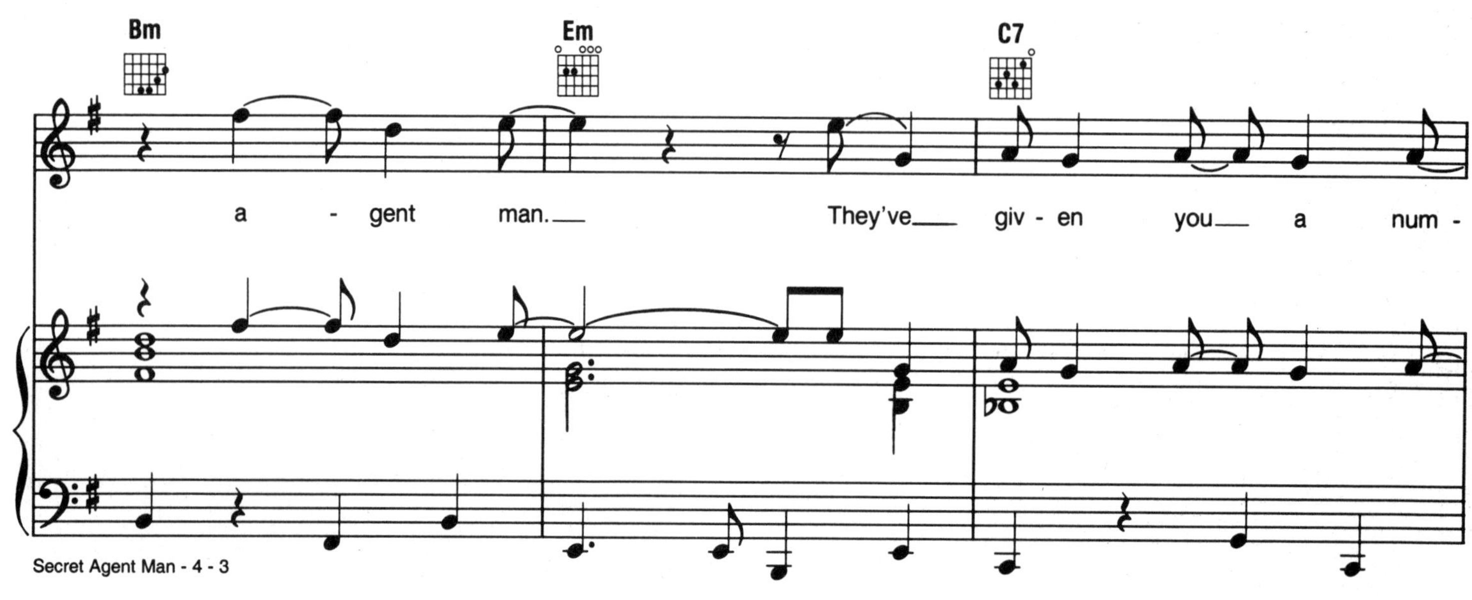
Bm
Em
C7
a - gent man. They've giv - en you a num -

B7
Em
C/E
ber and ta - ken 'way your name.
Em6
C/E
Em
C/E
1
Em6
C/E
2,3
Em6
C/E
4
Em6
C/E
2. Be -
Em6
C/E
Em6
C/E
Em

SHE'S NOT THERE

Words and Music by
ROD ARGENT

Bridge:
Am
F
A
D/F♯
F
how man-y peo - ple cried.
though they all knew.
1.2. But it's too (3.) late to say you're
cresc.
mf
Am
Em7
Am
D/F♯
F
sor-ry; how would I know? Why should I care? Please don't both - er try'n' to find
C
E7
her; she's not there.
Well, let me tell you 'bout the
cresc.
Chorus:
Am
D
Am
F
Am
D
way she looked, the way she act - ed, the col-or of her hair; her voice was
ff

Am
F
Am
D
A
soft and cool, her eyes were clear and bright, but she's not there.
1.
2.
To Next Strain
3.
Fine
N.C.
N.C.
N.C.
Am
D6
mp
f
(Inst. solo ad lib....
Am7
D6
Am
D6
Am7
D6
Am
D6
Am7
D6
Am
D6
A
D.S. 𝄋 al Fine
...end solo) 3. But it's too

SUNNY AFTERNOON

Words and Music by
RAY DAVIES

Dm
D7
SUN-NY AFT - ER - NOON.
SUN-NY AFT - ER - NOON.
Save me, save me,
Help me, help me,
G7
C7
save me from this squeeze,
help me sail a - way,
I've got a big fat mom-ma
You give me two good rea - sons
F
A7
Dm
tryin' to break me.
why I ought to stay.
And
'Cause
I love to live so
G9
Dm
G7
C7
F
pleas-ant - ly,
Live this life of lux - u - ry,
Laz - ing on a

A7
Dm
Dm7
Dm6
B♭
SUN-NY AFT - ER - NOON,
In sum - mer - time,
In sum-mer - time,
In sum-mer - time,
to Coda
1.
2.
2. My
Ah
D.S. al Coda
CODA
In sum-mer - time,
In sum-mer - time.
(Tacet)
Repeat and fade

SINCE I FELL FOR YOU

Words and Music by
BUDDY JOHNSON

Eb Eb6 Ab6 4fr. Bbm7 Eb Eb6 Ab 4fr. Ebm 6fr. Ab 4fr. Abm6
Love bringssuch mis-er-y and pain, I know I'll nev-er be the same
Gb F7 Bb7 Eb Emaj7 Eb Ebm7 Ab7 4fr. Ebm7 Ab7 4fr.
SINCE I FELL FOR YOU. It's too bad, it's too sad But
Ebm7 Ab7 4fr. Ebm7 Ab9 4fr. Eb Ebm7 Ab7 4fr. Ebm7 Ab7 4fr. Eb Gm 3fr. Cm7 3fr.
I'm in love with you, You love me then snub me, oh what can I do I'm
Fm9 F9 Bb7 Eb Eb6 Ab6 4fr. Bbm7 Eb Eb6 Ab 4fr. Ebm 6fr.
still in love with you; I guess I'll nev-er see the light, I get the blues most ev-'ry
Ab 4fr. Abm6 Gb F7 Bb7 1. Eb Cm7 3fr. F7 Bb7 2. Eb Emaj7 Gb Emaj7 Eb Eb6/9
night SINCE I FELL FOR YOU. YOU.

THIS DIAMOND RING

Words and Music by
BOB BRASS, AL KOOPER
and IRWIN LEVINE

F
D♭7
G♭
B♭m
thing.
me.
This dia-mond ring does-n't
This dia-mond ring can
E♭m
G♭
E♭m
G♭
B♭m
shine for me an-y-more, And this dia-mond ring does-n't
be some-thing beau-ti-ful, And this dia-mond ring can be
E♭m
G♭
G♭+
E♭m
B♭m
mean what it meant be-fore, So if you've got some-
dreams that are com-ing true, And then your heart won't
E♭m
B♭m
A♭m7
one whose love is true,
have to break like mine did,

D♭7
G♭
Let it shine for you.
If there's love be - hind it.
G
G7
Dm7
G7
C
E♭
Who wants to buy this dia - mond
F
Cm
Repeat and Fade
ring?

THIS MAGIC MOMENT

Words and Music by
DOC POMUS and
MORT SHUMAN

Gm
Eb
took me by sur - prise. I knew that you felt it, too
By the
F7
3
no chord
Gm
look in your eyes,
Sweet - er than
wine,
Soft - er than a
Eb
Bb
sum-mer night.
Ev - 'ry - thing I want I have
When - ev - er I
F7
no chord
Bb
hold you tight.
This mag - ic mo - ment,
while your

Gm
lips are close to mine, Will last for - ev - er,
Eb
For -
F7
ev - er, till the end of time.
Bb
Oh.
Gm
Oh.
Eb
Oh.
1. F7
no chord
This mag - ic
2. F7
Oh.
Bb

TRAINS AND BOATS AND PLANES

Words by
HAL DAVID

Music by
BURT BACHARACH

way, a - way from me.
C
We were so in love, and high a - bove we had a star
mp
F
to wish up - on. Wishes and dreams come true,
C
but not for me.
Am
The trains and the boats and planes took you a -
3
3

Am7
way, a - way from me.
You are from an -
f
D
Am7
D
oth - er part of the world.
You had to go back a -
Am7
D
Am7
while and then
you said you
soon would re - turn a - gain.
D
F
G
I'm wait - ing
here like I prom-ised to.
I'm wait - ing here, but

2nd time fade out
tacet
C
F
Am
Tacet
where are you?
Trains and boats and planes took you a - way,
but ev - 'ry time I see them I pray,
and if my prayers
can cross the sea
the trains and the boats and planes
will bring you back,
back home to me.
p
mp
3

WALK ON BY

Words by
HAL DAVID

Music by
BURT BACHARACH

With a beat

mf

Am7 D Am7 D

1. If you see me walk - in' down the street and I start to cry___ each time we meet,
2. I just can't get o - ver los - in' you and so if I seem___ bro - ken and blue,

Am7 D Gm7 Am7 Gm7

Walk on by,___ Walk on by.___

Am7 Dm Am7

Make be - lieve___ that you don't see the tears. Just let me grieve___ in
Fool - ish pride,___ that's all that I have left. So let me hide___ the

B♭
C
Fmaj7
pri - vate, 'Cause each time I see you, I break down and cry.
tears and the sad - ness you gave me when you said good - bye.
B♭
Fmaj7
B♭
Walk on by, Don't stop, Walk on by.
Fmaj7
B♭
1. Fmaj7
Don't stop, Walk on by.
B♭
2. Fmaj7

RUNAWAY

Words and Music by
DEL SHANNON and
MAX CROOK

D♭
C7
geth - er while our hearts_ were young.
Chorus
F
Dm
I'm a - walk - in' in the rain.__ Tears are fall - in' and I
F
feel a pain,____ A - wish - in' you were here by me__
Dm
F
To end this mis - er - y.__ And I won - der, wo - wo - wo - wo -

Dm
F
won - der
why,
why - why - why - why -
Dm
F
why she ran a - way, And I won - der where she will
C7
C7
C7sus4
F
B♭
stay,
My lit - tle run - a - way,
run - run - run - run -
1. F
C7
2. F
run - a - way.
run - a - way.

WHAT THE WORLD NEEDS NOW IS LOVE

Words by
HAL DAVID

Music by
BURT BACHARACH

Em7
C6
3rd time to Coda
B
love, No, not just for some, but for ev - 'ry - one.
B7
Em7
Lord, we don't need an - oth - er moun - tain,
Lord, we don't need an - oth - er mead - ow,
Dm9
G9/6
There are moun - tains and hill - sides e -
There are corn - fields and wheat - fields e -
Cmaj7
C6
Dm7
nough to climb; There are o - ceans and
nough to grow; There are sun - beams and

G9/6
Cmaj7
Em7
riv - ers e - nough to cross, E - nough to last
moon - beams e - nough to shine, Oh, lis - ten, Lord,
A7
D9
Am7/D
till the end of time.
if you want to know. What the
Coda
B
B7
E7
C6
C
ev - 'ry-one.
No, not just for some, Oh, but
Bm7
Cmaj7
D7
G
just for ev - 'ry - one.

YOU DON'T OWN ME

Words and Music by
JOHN MADARA and DAVE WHITE

2
B♭
boys.
stay.
And
I
don't
tell
me
what to do,
don't
tell
you
what to say,
Gm
Don't
tell
me
I
don't
tell
you
E♭
what to say;
what to do;
And
please
when I go
So
just
let me

F7
out with you,
be my-self,
Don't
That's
put
all
me
I
To Coda
Bbm
D.S. al Coda
on dis-play.
ask of you.
'Cause,
You
don't
CODA
Bb
I'm
young
and
I
Gm
love to be young,
I'm
free
and
I

Eb

love to be free; ___ To live my

life the way that I want, ___ To

F7

say and do what - ev - er I please. ___

Bbm Ebm F7 Repeat and Fade

___ You don't own me. ___

OH, PRETTY WOMAN

Words and Music by
ROY ORBISON and BILL DEES

F
Dm
Bb
WO - MAN I could - n't help but see, PRET - TY WO - MAN that you look
C7
love - ly as can be Are you lone - ly just like me?
Bbm
PRET - TY WO - MAN
Eb7
Ab
Fm
Bbm
stop a - while, PRET - TY WO - MAN talk a - while, PRET - TY WO - MAN
Eb7
Ab
Bbm
Eb7
give your smile to me PRET - TY WO - MAN yeah, yeah, yeah

Ab
Fm
Bbm
Eb7
Ab
PRET-TY WO-MAN look my way,
PRET-TY WO-MAN say you'll stay with me
F7
Dm
Bbm
C7
F
Dm
'Cause I need you
I'll treat you right
Come to me ba - by
Bbm
C7
Be mine to - night
PRET-TY
F
Dm
F
Dm
WO-MAN don't walk on by,
PRET - TY WO - MAN don't make me cry,
PRET - TY
Bb
C7
WO-MAN don't walk a - way
Hey,
O. K.

If that's the way it must be, O. K.
I guess I'll go on home, it's
late There'll be to-mor-row night, but wait! What do I see
Is she walk-ing back to me?
Yeah, she's walk-ing back to me!
OH,
1 F
2 F
PRET-TY WO-MAN
PRET-TY WO-MAN

YOU'RE SIXTEEN

Words and Music by
RICHARD M. SHERMAN and
ROBERT B. SHERMAN

C
Am7
D7
G9
G7
C
F
shine. You're six - teen you're beau - ti - ful and you're mine.
C
G7
C
You're my ba - by, you're my pet. We fell in love on the
D9
night we met. You touched my hand, my heart went 'pop', And
G6(add9)
G9
G6(add9)
C
ooh, when we kissed we could not stop, You walked out of my dreams,

E7
F
C
Am7
into my arms, now you're my angel divine. You're sixteen,
D7
1
G9
G7
Am
Dm7
G6(add9)
you're beautiful and you're mine.
Ooh, you come
2
B7
B♭7
A7
beautiful and you're mine. Ooh you're
beautiful, You're sixteen and you're mine.

IT'S OVER

Words and Music by
ROY ORBISON and BILL DEES

Em
F
Em
It breaks your heart in two
to know she's
F
Em
F
3
been un-true.
But oh, what will you do
when she says to
G7
F
G7
F
G7
you, "There's some - one new, we're through,
we're through.
It's
C
Em
G7
C
o - ver,
it's o - ver,
it's o - ver."
F
All the rain-bows in the sky
start to weep, then say, "Good-

Am
C7
F
C7
bye." You won't be see - ing rain-bows an-y more.
F
Set-ting suns be-fore they fall ech-o to you, "That's all, that's
Am
Dm
B♭
G7
C7
all." But you'll see lone - ly sun-sets af-ter all
3
3
it's o - ver, it's o - ver, it's o - ver, it's
F
1.
2.
o - ver. ver.

80 Years of Popular Music

80 80 Years of Popular Music

80

AD0154

80 Years

The Sixties

Piano/Vocal/Chords
(MF9827)
ISBN 0-7692-6725-4 UPC 0-29156-95406-7

Titles in this 82-song collection include: **Aquarius/Let the Sun Shine In • Bad Moon Rising • California Girls • (Sittin' On) The Dock of the Bay • The House of the Rising Sun • I Got You Babe • I Saw Her Standing There • In-A-Gadda-Da-Vida • Itsy Bitsy Teeny Weenie Yellow Polka Dot Bikini • Mony, Mony • Oh, Pretty Woman • Raindrops Keep Fallin' on My Head • Soul Man • When a Man Loves a Woman • White Rabbit • Wipe Out** and more.

The Seventies

Piano/Vocal/Chords
(MF9828)
ISBN 0-7692-6985-0 UPC 0-29156-95704-4

Titles in this 58-song collection include: **Baby I Love Your Way • Didn't I Blow Your Mind This Time • Go Your Own Way • A Horse with No Name • Hotel California • If You Don't Know Me By Now • I'll Take You There • Killing Me Softly with His Song • Love Train • My Sharona • Old Time Rock & Roll • The Rose • Stairway to Heaven • Time in a Bottle • What a Fool Believes • You Are So Beautiful** and more.

The Eighties

80

Piano/Vocal/Chords
(MF9829)
ISBN 0-7692-6994-X UPC 0-29156-95742-6

Titles in this 55-song collection include: **Africa • Against All Odds (Take a Look at Me Now) • Arthur's Theme (Best That You Can Do) • Back in the High Life Again • Cuts Like a Knife • I Will Always Love You • In the Air Tonight • Like a Rock • Man in the Mirror • On the Wings of Love • (I've Had) The Time of My Life • Up Where We Belong • What's Love Got to Do with It • Words Get in the Way** and more.

The Nineties

Piano/Vocal/Chords
(MF9830)
ISBN 0-7692-7103-0 UPC 0-29156-95950-5

Titles in this 58-song collection include: **All I Wanna Do • All My Life • Because You Loved Me • Foolish Games • I Believe I Can Fly • (Everything I Do) I Do It for You • I Don't Want to Miss a Thing • I Love You Always Forever • I Swear • I'll Be There for You (Theme from "Friends") • Kiss from a Rose • MMMBop • Quit Playing Games with My Heart • Sunny Came Home • Tears in Heaven • Un-Break My Heart • Walking on the Sun • You're Still the One** and more.